Bengal Engineer

Alfred Harris Vaux (1828–1873),
aged 26. 'Bengal Engineer'.

Bengal Engineer

EDITED BY PETER VAUX

The Pentland Press
Edinburgh – Cambridge – Durham – USA

First published in 1994
by The Pentland Press Ltd
1 Hutton Close
South Church
Bishop Auckland
Durham

British Library Cataloguing in Publication Data
A catalogue record for this book is available from the British Library.

ISBN 1–85821-210-3

Jacket illustration details the East Indian Railway locomotive
'Fairy Queen' (1855–1909) (New Dehli Rail Transport Museum), see page 193.

Typeset by Carnegie Publishing Ltd, 18 Maynard St, Preston
Printed and bound by Antony Rowe Ltd, Chippenham

For Alfred Vaux's
great-great-grandchildren,
Frances, Carleton, Alexander, Benedict
Deepahk and Hugo

CONTENTS

FOREWORD

By Sir Peter Parker, KBE, LVO

Railways', in the words of that fighting Victorian, General Roberts of Kandahar, 'were good civilisers as well as defenders of Indian security, vital to civil as well as military administration.' Actually, the rail system there was slow to develop because of lack of funding – not an unusual constraint here in the UK in my experience. But the Indian network was gradually built up and extraordinary feats were performed to achieve it, making unsung heroes of many good railwaymen.

Peter Vaux in this vivid collection of letters gives history a fascinating human focus. History usually comes at us in great sweeps of generalisation. Here we have the personal saga of a railway engineer who became Chief Engineer to the East India Railway, the line running north from Calcutta roughly along the Ganges towards Cawnpore. The mosaic of letters presents the story of the pioneering of the railway system which was to prove perhaps the most durable of legacies of Empire to Republic.

So much shines through the domestic detail of the correspondence of Alfred Vaux and his wife. First, the sheer technical triumph of the work in hand. This was the age of heroic engineering, what Lord Curzon as Viceroy described as 'the all conquering influence of steam'.

Secondly, the sheer endurance, dedication and courage of Vaux and his family is awesome. Consider the calm, good humour in a harrowing letter to his mother in August 1857 – he reports on 'the unpleasant details of India', and he goes on to tell of the agonizing events around the Indian Mutiny. Then he ends, 'while we are surrounded with sorrow and yesterday's horror is only equalled by the account of today's atrocity, it does our hearts good to hear of your quiet life.' His wife in 1862 writes with passion about 'this unhealthy climate, running risks every hour of our lives'; she is so enraged by the gossip in England that her family was living luxuriously, she punctures the paper with her pen.

Thirdly, I find myself reading between the lines a story of exceptional management leadership. I have come to learn that the construction and running of railways is a challenge which gives people the chance to give the best of themselves. It seems to have drawn the best out of the Editor's extraordinary grandfather. As another railwayman, George Stephenson, said: 'the most difficult engineering is the engineering of man.'

Breathes there a railwayman with soul so dead who will not be transported by this remarkable record?

Peter Parker
Chairman British Railways Board
1976–1983

PREFACE

IN 1948 my Uncle Alfred left me a black tin box containing many interesting family papers; amongst them was a battered cardboard box in which was a daunting collection of what looked like Air Mail letters, written in sometimes faded black ink on flimsy pink, blue or white paper—some of these folded sheets being almost identical in size, shape and function to our own contemporary aerograms. All were rolled up very tightly and tied with string so that, when unfolded, the bundles immediately sprang back like frightened hedgehogs. I quickly put them away again, promising to read them properly when I had more time. I did not reopen the box until 1984 when, having received a further packet of similar letters, I felt I should get something done. The first task was to flatten the papers so that they could be read without their pinching one's fingers and the second actually to read and sort them into chronological context. This last was not so easy, as the date-lines often omitted the year. I eventually found that I had a collection of letters from a Railway Engineer of the East India Company covering almost twenty years, from a junior position to that of Under-Secretary of State. They were written to his mother, his sisters and, later, to the children who had been sent home to school in England. There were also some from his first and second wives, but some of these were only just decipherable, being closely 'cross-written' as was the custom of the time. However, taken together, all these letters provide a most interesting description of life in India between 1856 and 1873. In assembling these extracts I have edited out many of the references to purely domestic details of friends and relations at home.

Alfred Vaux had good handwriting, when he chose to apply it, so that some of the letters have been reproduced in their original state, especially where he had included little sketches. In others the shaking hand of fever was all too apparent. He could never have guessed that they would be typed out by his grandson, for his great- and great-great-grandchildren to read.

P.A.L.V.
Fleet
Hants, England

INTRODUCTION

ALFRED HARRIS VAUX was born in his father's surgery in Pudding Lane in the City of London on 25 June 1828. His mother recorded that his weight at one week old was 8lb. 8¼oz. and that by the age of twelve he had suffered from measles, scarlet fever and small-pox. He was the son of Calvert Bowyer Vaux, a surgeon practising in Pudding Lane, who had been born in Birmingham and was the last of a line of doctors dating back to the time of Cromwell. In fact, between the mid-seventeenth century and Calvert's death in 1833, the family had produced at least eight doctors, all Quakers, practising in Reigate, Birmingham or London. The Pudding Lane practice had been in the family for over a hundred years but, after Calvert, there were no more doctors—except for one cousin—and Calvert himself turned back to the Church of England, all his children being baptised in St Benet's Church, Gracechurch Street, in the City of London.

Dr Calvert Vaux died in 1833, at the age of forty-two, so by the time these letters begin the widow had been coping for sixteen years as she launched her six children into the world. She was Emily Brickwood, who came from a family of merchants trading in the East Indies and the South Seas. Her brother, John Brickwood, was a great standby to her and, in particular, was to prove influential in launching the young Alfred on his career as a civil engineer. It seems possible that he helped Alfred secure an appointment with the East India Company.

Alfred Vaux was educated at Merchant Taylor's School, leaving at the age of sixteen to enter King's College, London, where for four years he trained as a scientific engineer. This was followed by a further three years gaining practical experience at various engineering works and construction sites, among these the Great Exhibition Building in Hyde Park. His training complete, his first appointment was in Dublin, under Mr William Dargan, where he was engaged from 1851 until 1855 in large construction work for the Irish Railways.

On 9 April 1855 Alfred married Emily Williams who, like himself, was aged twenty-seven. She was the sister of John Williams who had married Alfred's sister Emily in 1851 and, again like Alfred, was the daughter of a City of London doctor. Soon after this Alfred joined the East Indian Railway—then part of the East India Company—and sailed for India in the autumn of that year. He arrived in Calcutta, at that time the centre of Government, in February 1856 and was sent up the Ganges to Rajmahal. His wife, having given birth to a son, Brickwood, took her baby out to join her husband in January 1857. She was just in time for the Indian Mutiny.

The family lived at first in the rather dreary and very unhealthy Rajmahal but later in the more cheerful riverside village of Suffrabad, near Monghyr, until some time in 1863, when they moved down to Calcutta—presumably on Alfred's promotion to head office. By June 1865 Emily had borne six children, of whom two had been sent home to England and one had died in infancy. They had all suffered almost continuous illness, and Emily had had in addition at least two miscarriages; she also developed a heart condition, which became steadily worse.

In June 1865, however, the parents and the three remaining children sailed for home leave in England—Alfred had had none for ten years, although his wife had been home once to take the two older children. Emily died as the ship passed through the Red Sea and was buried overboard. She was thirty-seven. Father and the three children, of course, continued the voyage to Southampton, arriving in July. On 4 August the youngest boy died in Croydon at the age of 366 days. Leaving the children with relatives, Alfred returned alone to India in February 1866—the same month in which he was admitted to the Institute of Civil Engineers.

He was back again by October 1867, however, for on the 27th he married Caroline Hollins in Croydon. The following July he and his new wife had passed Aden, *en route* for India, and on 25 August their first child was born in Calcutta. He died seven months later. Caroline is described on her marriage certificate as 'of full age', and her photographs of that time show her to have been in her early twenties. The daughter of an organist, now dead, and herself a music teacher, there are indications that she did not find favour with her mother-in-law, who is not shown as a witness at the wedding. At any rate, she seems to have coped well in Calcutta, producing two more sons, one of whom was my father, Charles Alfred Vaux, and yet a third who was born in Simla in March 1872 but died in Calcutta the following December.

By 1870 Alfred had become senior enough to move with the Government from the capital in Calcutta to Simla during the summer months, although the wives seem to have gone a few weeks ahead of their husbands, living up in the hills alone with their servants and children. Kipling, in his *Plain Tales from the Hills*, made much of immoral conduct between these grass widows and single officers on leave. My father told me that his mother and her friends regarded Kipling as a scoundrel who wrote these scandalous stories for the sake of sensation and the money they brought him. If so, he would not have been the only journalist to do that.

Alfred's last letter, to his daughter Susan, was written from Simla on 8 September 1873. He died there on 16 October, of cholera, at the age of forty-five. Caroline lost no time in packing up and leaving India with her two little boys, Percy (four) and Charlie (three), for she was already four months pregnant. Her youngest son, Julian, was to be born in Richmond on 13 March 1874.

At the end of this book there is, together with the maps, an extract from Alfred's pedigree showing his immediate family, most of whom are mentioned in his letters. There is in the Epilogue a brief account of what happened to them all. It is of note that of the thirteen children fathered by Alfred Vaux, either born or miscarried, seven survived to adulthood; only two of the males and neither of the females had progeny and only one of these had any sons.

PART I

I

EARLY DAYS

WHEN Alfred had finished his theoretical training at King's College, London, he worked for eighteen months in the drawing offices of Messrs Walker & Burges. Feeling then the need for practical experience at shop-floor level, he wrote to his uncle for advice. John Brickwood's reply is the earliest letter in the box.

> South Seas House, London
> 21 Dec 1849
>
> Dear Alfred,
>
> Consequent upon a conversation with Mr Walker to-day I wish you to call on me here as soon after 12 tomorrow as you can.
>
> Truly yours,
> J. O. Brickwood.

This led to a year's very hard physical work in the iron foundry of Messrs Fox & Henderson at London Works in Birmingham. Mr Walker, however, kept an eye on his former pupil and eleven months later wrote to Mr Brickwood.

> Birmingham, 25 Nov 1850
>
> My dear John,
>
> As the Christmas holidays approach would it not be agreeable to Vaux's family to have him near them?

Does not the fixing up of the 'Glass Palace' give a good opportunity for this and for practice at the same time?

Would not <u>Fox</u> readily transport <u>Vaux</u> if you were to give him the hint?

If you approve, better name it to V– first and get his opinion—he may be at present engaged upon something that is interesting and useful. I did not think that this was much the case when I saw him but the work was <u>strengthening</u> and developing his <u>muscular</u> formation.

I remain, my dear John,
very truly,
Bob Walker.

John Brickwood was swift to take action.

South Seas House, London
6 Dec 1850

Dear Alfred,

Mr Walker has written to me the enclosed very kind and considerate letter & I wrote and thanked him for it.

I sent it to your excellent mother for perusal and she seems pleased with the idea of your coming to London. On Mr Walker's suggestion I have spoken to Mr Fox—also to Mr Henderson on your behalf—and both these gentlemen have expressed their willingness to allow you to be at the Great Building in the Park during the remainder of the time occupied in its completion.

Mr Henderson very obligingly said he would either write to you to that effect or see you when at the 'London Works' on Saturday or Monday.

I am disposed to think it a most valuable opportunity for you to obtain knowledge of the means of putting materials together on a large scale for the construction of the most Extraordinary Building ever made—with the additional advantage (if you avail yourself of the opportunity) of enabling you to say hereafter that you had been allowed to assist in the construction of that building.

If you see Mr Henderson perhaps you will express your feeling of obligation to him and Mr Fox and shew a zeal to be useful as Superintendent or Clerk of Works or in any manner in which they may permit you to aid in carrying out the Plans at the same time as you will be acquiring knowledge in your profession; although not at so early a period, feeling yourself entitled to any pecuniary remuneration.

Your affectionate Uncle,
J. Brickwood.

Your letter to me of the 26 Nov partly encouraged me to see Messrs Fox and Henderson and speak to them as above related.

The Great Exhibition of 1851, of which the Prince Consort was the main driving force, was the first of those major international industrial exhibitions which have today become quite common. The centre-piece was the Great Exhibition Building in Hyde Park. This huge edifice, the height of a cathedral and with a massive domed tower in the centre, was constructed entirely of glass supported on a delicate cast-iron framework; it was so immense as easily to encompass some of the largest trees growing in the Park. Such a project naturally capturing the popular imagination, it became known as 'The Crystal Palace'. After the Exhibition it was dismantled and re-erected on a hill at Sydenham where it remained, a feature of London and visible for miles, until destroyed in a spectacular fire in 1936.

For about a year Alfred was glad to work for next to nothing in order to gain experience of such construction methods. When

Dr Calvert Bowyer Vaux (1792–1833),
Alfred's father, aged 38.

the building was nearing completion he approached his uncle for assistance in finding a more lucrative position. His letter described his professional career up to January 1851.

Gt Exhibition Building,
Hyde Park, London.
1st January 1851

My dear Sir,

The object I have in mind while writing this letter is to lay before you a somewhat detailed account of my education and employment as an Engineer up to the present time when I am almost 23 years old, and to obtain your further assistance in advancing my prospects now that I may fairly consider my period of pupillage to have ended.

In 1844, at the age of 16, I was entered as a student in the Engineering Department of King's College, London, and immediately began to practise surveying under the superintendence of Mr Castle, a practical gentleman who had been boundary surveyor in Canada. To this I devoted considerable time and became sufficiently skilful to be employed by him in the autumn of the following year in taking the levels of several of the railway lines then proposed. In the beginning of the year 1846 I returned to King's College and continued my studies there. These included Geometrical Drawing, Mathematics, the Laws of Mechanics, Natural Philosophy, Manufactures and in fact all the elements of all those branches of knowledge which may be supposed useful to the Scientific Engineer. Having completed the usual course at King's College, with your kind introduction, I became in June 1848 a pupil of Messrs Walker & Burges, and almost immediately was sent into the Middle Bedford Level to take sections and borings to ascertain the nature of the soil on which the extensive

Mrs Emily Vaux (née Brickwood) (1792–1881),
Alfred's mother, aged 38.

Drainage operations have since been carried out. On my return to Gt George St. I was engaged for several months in assisting in getting out the contract drawings, and preparing estimates for these works. During the time I was in this office, I was occupied principally in drawing and estimating. In the summer of 1849 I was sent to Dover where, besides the Admiralty Pier, forming part of the proposed Harbour of Refuge, other very extensive harbour works were being carried out. At Christmas 1849, thinking that although my employment in Messrs Walker & Burges Office and upon their works was of a very varied and improving character, it did not give the practical knowledge of detail and the strengths of materials which is so requisite, I determined upon following if possible the advice of Mr Walker by passing a year in Manual Work in a foundry. You kindly procured me this opportunity by introducing me to Messrs Fox & Henderson and early in 1850 I went to the London Works Nr Birmingham. While there I worked consecutively in the Pattern Shop, Foundry, Smithy and Fitting Shop, both at fine work and rough heavy jobs and at all times took my turn with the other men. Among the many advantages that I enjoyed there were seeing and assisting in making two large Light Houses which I had previously been employed upon in Messrs W & B Office. I also assisted in casting many of the bridges for the Gt Northn Railway and in fitting and testing the ironwork of the Gt Exh Building. In Dec I came to this building where I am now occupied in superintending part of the fixing. As our work here is drawing towards a close I am very anxious to obtain a remuneratory employment. With reference to my past conduct I may with confidence refer to Messrs Walker & Burges, Messrs Fox & Henderson, and Mr Castle. If you will further my object you may depend upon my zeal diligence and regularity and you will confer another lasting obligation upon

My dear Sir

Ever your obed Nephew,

Alfred H. Vaux.

J. J. Brickwood Esq

This letter apparently brought results, there being evidence that for the next couple of years Alfred worked in the Office of the Industrial Exhibition in Dublin. There is a note from the Engineer's Office, City Hall, Dublin, addressed to A. H. Vaux, Great Industrial Building, Dublin, apologising for not forwarding some correspondence.

The last letter in the box from this period was written by John Brickwood.

South Seas House

London—4 July 1853

Dear Alfred,

I am glad to observe by your letter that in the completion of Mr Dargan's great Dublin Work you have a prospect of its leading you to being entrusted by him with further employment.

This is quite in accordance with his manner of expressing himself in reference to you when I last saw him here a few weeks back. From what he then said I have no doubt of its being in your power to increase the confidence he seemed disposed to place in you and that you may become more and more useful to him in the important works he is in the habit of undertaking.

Respecting your Brother James I am puzzled. I should be glad to aid in your mother's anxiety in regard to him but I know not how to do so. As to aiding him in earning a livelihood I see no prospect of having it in my power & I cannot hold out a hope to that effect. I have received the half note you have kindly sent for him & and I shall be willing to confer with your mother as to the best mode of applying it for his benefit. I have hoped that either you or Calvert might think of something for him. If you forward the other ½ note I will keep the £10 until the expression of your mother's wish regarding it.

Sincerely yours

J. J. Brickwood.

Alfred did indeed stay on with Mr Dargan, working on the Irish Railways, until some time in 1855. On 9 April of that year he married Emily Williams and by December he had sailed for Calcutta.

The reference to Alfred's brother James is intriguing. This shadowy figure flits through subsequent correspondence, usually because someone or other has become anxious about him. All that can be discovered is that he was two years older than Alfred and that he died in New Zealand, but when is not known—he may have become a sailor. Calvert was the eldest of the brothers, but the previous year he had emigrated to the USA, where he was starting to make his name as a landscape architect, so would hardly have had time to help James.

2

PASSAGE TO INDIA

In the December of 1855 Alfred, now aged twenty-seven, was on his way to Calcutta to join the East Indian Railway. His wife was to follow him a year later.

By that time, the voyage via the Cape of Good Hope had fallen into disuse for passenger traffic, although of course freighters still went that way, what was known as the 'overland route' having been introduced in 1830. Passengers sailed from Southampton to Alexandria, where they disembarked and continued by coach—or, later, railway—to the port of Suez, where they joined another ship for either Bombay or Calcutta. The schedule usually permitted a few days in Cairo, where passengers stayed at Shepheards Hotel, visited the Pyramids and bought a certain amount of hot weather clothing. The Suez Canal was not opened until 1869.

Alfred's ship, the *Pera*, made an unscheduled call at Lisbon, where he wrote to his wife Emily and to his mother.

In Quarantine in the Tagus
Friday 11 January 1856

My dear Mother,

I have just posted a letter to Emily and sent it via Madrid, postage unpaid, upon which the dear girl will doubtless have to pay an alarming postage. The confounded Portuguese and Spanish authorities do not recognise our Queen's stamps. I am very glad of the opportunity to write for if she heard of the dirty weather we have had she might have been anxious.

I write to you now in expectation of the regular mail steam ship which has been delayed three days and will probably be in the river tonight.

You do not I know imagine where I am for after reading the brilliant account in the *Times* of the trial trip of the *Pera*, who would imagine that in a gale on Thursday one of the Engines thoroughly broke down 'and there we were all that day in the Bay of Biscay' with a westerly wind blowing. It was quite as much as we could do guided by the admirable seamanship of Captain Day to keep off the coast, for the spars and tackle broke when the sails were set.

This morning however as the haze cleared off the Atlantic the Bar of Cintra and the Rock of Lisbon were seen rioting as it were on the surface. We signalled for a Pilot and a most romantic individual in a variegated shirt and yellow shoes, came on board and took us up the river through the clear atmosphere and balmy air of this beautiful place. The sun is warm and the feeling is like the calmest summer weather in England.

All passengers decorated themselves in shore going attire, but were for to-day disappointed. A gentleman died on board of Bronchitis on Wednesday and the Portuguese authorities are timid—for the present they refuse to allow us to go ashore and the yellow quarantine flag still flaps lazily at our masthead—to-morrow we hope to receive permission, and content ourselves tonight with eating oranges and listening to our band.

I fear we are not thankful enough to the Almighty hand which has allowed 250 of us to reach safe port after really considerable danger. We do not know how long the Engineers require for refitting their crippled machinery but probably two or three days will be necessary. It is not unlikely that we may

17

be detained until the Marseilles (of the 10th January) Mail has left Malta—in which case we shall have to stop in Egypt for another week. At this season a few days at Grand Cairo would be interesting, but the delay to many is most serious, especially to officers returning after furlough and to the Chinese traders.

You cannot think how you have all been thought of by me while we were tossing about the bay in the late gale—in the intervals of sea sickness, the contrast of your nice cheerful room to my close densely peopled cupboard of a cabin constantly occurred to me.

Altogether I suffered very little and only kept my bed for one day. Two or three days head ache followed and after that a good appetite—such a one as would gain me credit even in your dear masticating circle.

Give my best love to all and believe me your affect. Son

Alfred H. Vaux.

Disappointingly, there are no letters from Egypt, where Alfred transferred to the P & O ship *Hindoostan*. However, from Aden he wrote to his favourite sister Julia. She was now aged twenty-five but seems to have been crippled, for there are several references to her being in pain from 'rheumatism'—more likely arthritis. She died at the age of forty-one, still a spinster.

Aden—

Monday—

My dear Julia,

We are lying in Aden Harbour and taking in 500 tons of coal to carry us to Ceylon. It is a poor place but of course I went on shore this morning to see it and galloped about 4 miles out to the military cantonments on a donkey, and back before breakfast—made a breakfast off Curried buffalo's hump

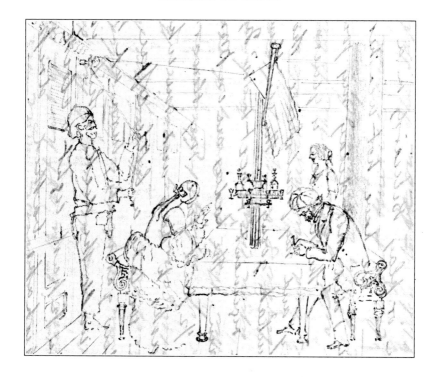

Shipboard scene.

and water, idled about, bought some light trousers at the Parsee shop and paid an exorbitant price for them and came on board early leaving the rest to have races in the broiling sun or play billiards in a cool room there is in the Hotel. We have hot weather now and I am very pleased that I did not delay my journey till the cool season was over. The Red Sea is generally the hottest part of the journey and my frontispiece shows part of our saloon with a *punkah* going. The gentleman is a Captain Norton in the same regiment as and next to Mr Tyrrell whom I knew in Birmingham. The ladies are on promotion.

In the morning about ½ past five my steward comes into

our cabin and asks Dr Kay and me whether we will take tea or coffee—we take a little coffee and jump up, put on a very few garments, turn up the lowest to our knees and walk the deck while it is being washed. Before the ½ past eight o'clock breakfast we have shaved, bathed, dressed and made ourselves a little fit to associate with Ladies—after breakfast we converse until the sun gets very hot when we retire to the after part of the ship where an awning is strained, or we descend to the saloon and do anything that cannot be interrupted by the presence of a lot of people. The stewards pull the *punkahs* whenever the passengers may require them. The whole crew is composed of Sepoys and Chinese and at night they lie about the ship in every direction with very little clothing upon them. We have Arabs, Nubians and as queer a lot of fellows as you could find anywhere and they pitch into an immense amount of rice and ghee—the latter is rank clarified butter and smells atrociously.

The days are delightful about sunrise and the nights are very clear. There is a piano on board and it is surprising that it sounds as well as it does. After dinner and tea a quiet rubber finishes the evening—sixteen points are the highest.

To-day we lose the Bombay part of our passengers and those who have Indian friends receive letters—and how I wish I could hear from you—I think of my pretty rheumatic dear sister constantly and long to know if she and my respectable wife love each other as much as they should.

Give my best love to Emily Newburgh and write me nice confiding letters never thinking of paying the postage—as soon as I can I will prepay mine but do not you trouble yourself about that, only write about yourselves.

Kiss dear Mother,
Ever your affect Brother
Alfred H. Vaux.

'Emily Newburgh' means Alfred's sister, Emily Williams, now with her husband John in Newburgh, USA.

Off Ceylon
20th February 1856

My dear Mother,

It may be a few weeks before I have another opportunity of sending you a letter so I write to tell you that tomorrow night we hope to reach Madras—which is within three days steaming of Calcutta. We shall all be heartily glad to escape from the confinement of ship board, although since our new Engines broke down off the coast of Spain we have had a delightful passage.

On Monday we landed for a few hours at Point de Galle in Ceylon and after a delicious breakfast of Plantains and fresh pineapples Norton Chapman and I took a coach and drove to Wak Woolei—about five miles up the country and caught there the first glimpse of true Indian scenery. The paddy fields on each side of the road were bounded by regular jungle and of course interested me. As was natural we feasted ourselves and suffered consequently. In the gardens of Wak Woolei we saw the snake charmers and all day long we were pestered by the natives who surrounded us offering jewels—tortoise shell ornaments and ebony nick nacks for sale. Their imitations of precious stones are excellent and many real jewels of surpassing beauty are to be purchased—only however by good judges. I bought a very pretty tortoise shell paper knife for Em and wasted two or three rupees but restrained myself rather more than I should have been able to do if I had been travelling homewards.

We left 30 of our passengers in Galle and took up some more bound for Calcutta. I certainly recognised one of them, a Captain Daly who has been ordered round from Bombay by Telegraph from Lord Dalhousie, but upon comparing notes can not discover where we have met. In Madras we leave Generals Foster and Armstrong and Colonel Haldane and his wife—all names that would be recognised by Harriet Cameron but of no interest to you.

We have on board an agreeable lot of officers and a pleasant Captain—Ironson by name, a near relative of the little boy who was shot by accident by a companion—concerning whom I wrote to you some years back from the South of Ireland.

You can scarcely conceive how I look forward to the receipt of home news—I want you to tell me how you all manage and whether my dear Em frets. Then I am not certain if they sent her the money rightly and altogether I am anxious for the first English letters which I expect to have in ten days or a fortnight. Many people on board the *Hindoostan* are fidgetting themselves and with some cause about the Small Pox. It has been in the ship since it left Calcutta and notwithstanding all precautions there have been many cases—three of the crew were left in the last port—the Doctor is recovering we heard. As yet none of the passengers have been touched—I do not fear it but am careful about diet, night air and so forth.

Captain Norgate who is with us has lived a considerable time on the line of railway and says the appointments are very good and the Engineers very pleasant fellows.

I am somewhat confused for the ship is rolling considerably and immediately opposite me is a party of Cadets at the Piano singing the 'Ratcatcher's Daughter' and other popular little ballads—but I retain sufficient control over my pen and brain to send you my dearest Mother my love—second only to that to my wife.

Your ever dutiful Son,
Alfred H. Vaux.

The *Hindoostan* duly docked at Calcutta in late February 1856, and Alfred at last received his long-awaited mail from England, but he was disappointed with the mere 'scrap' from his mother, which was enclosed in a letter from his wife. He remained only briefly in Calcutta—by 3 April he was writing from his permanent station of Rajmahal—but found time to send a note to his mother, probably just to let her know that he had arrived.

6th March 1856
Calcutta

My dear Mother,

Many thanks for your scrap enclosed in Emily's letter. I knew you would all be glad to hear from me so I wrote whenever an opportunity occurred not heeding the sixpences which I knew must be paid on delivering the letters. I was very glad to hear that Julia was improving and that you thought my dear wife looked tolerably well at Sutton. Long before this a final arrangement will have been made for her and I suppose that as the money is deducted from my salary it will be paid regularly to her order. I bank at the Oriental Bank in Calcutta and after a time I dare say I shall be able to send home some more ready money but at first I have many things to purchase. Rajmahal, my station, is amongst the Southals and there are very few Europeans in the neighbour-hood—it is impossible to purchase anything there beyond the simplest food so I have to take furniture up the River.

The hot season is coming on and after a slight cessation will last till October. It would be wrong for anyone to come out to India for the first time during the summer months, but if all goes well with my dear Em, I hope she may start in October.

Em writes in the most loving manner of you and Julia and I trust she deserves the kindness she receives from you and my dear pretty sister Katie too.

I am in good health and hope to maintain it amongst the jungles. The late Gov General leaves to-day for England and we have witnessed quite an impressive spectacle in his farewell.

I have hired a servant to go up the river with me—a Mussulman who is to perform the several duties of *Kitmulgar*, Bearer and *Moser*, which are the same as those of Table Servant, Valet and Tailor. His name is Hinguno—if he were a Hindu he would not touch my food. It is absolutely necessary to keep a tailor to mend as fast as the *dhoby* tears the shirts and trousers.

When my household is arranged I shall write you an acct.

> Ever your dutiful Son,
> Alfred H. Vaux.

3

RAJMAHAL

On 3 April 1856 Alfred told his sister Julia that he had been nearly two weeks in Rajmahal. If the voyage up the Ganges took about a week, he must have remained no more than a fortnight in Calcutta. About this time he received news that in January his brother-in-law John Williams, who had married his sister Emily in 1851, had died in the United States, where he had been working as an architect. Luckily, Alfred's elder brother Calvert—the landscape architect who was to design and lay out Central Park, New York—was already out there and was able to take care of Emily and her young son Cuthbert. One way and another, Alfred felt pretty gloomy as he wrote to his mother.

Rajmahal

3 April 1856

My dear Mother,

Your pen is too idle for the wishes of your son—I have heard tidings of a case awaiting my orders in Calcutta and will I dare say receive it in another fortnight or three weeks—perhaps in it may be a letter from you.

Thank you dear Mother for taking so much care of my wife—she told me of her visit to Tulse Hill and her not half liking the jaunt.

I have just received news of our dear sister Emily's loss and intend to write to her, dear earnest hearted good creature that she is. Cal will be kind and considerate to her I feel sure.

I am now suffering from boils and am quite low. The worst of the matter is that I get no pity for everyone tells me that those who have boils generally escape fever!

The natives in this neighbourhood are desperately sickly but Europeans from some cause or another stand the climate better than those who are born in it.

Yr Dutiful Son, Alfred.

There must have been a post going out that day for he also wrote to his sister Julia. As he always wrote cheerfully to her he did not mention his boils.

3 April 1856
Rajmahal

My dear Julia,

How is the Rheumatism, have you overcome its disagreeableness? I trust that you have recovered strength sufficient at any rate to write and tell me how you are and to give me your views of home affairs. You asked me before leaving England to write home good accounts of what I saw and did, not thinking that you knew all about the Overland Route and kindred matters. I think I have obeyed you.

I have lived nearly a fortnight in Rajmahal and have done a great deal of work in the time but have looked about a little too, just to notice the differences between English life and this.

On the 20th March the steamer *James Hume* paddled to the side of the River Ganges and your brother and his acquaintance Taylor, the Indigo Planter, walked ashore on a plank laid from the bulwarks to the clayey bank. We scrambled up a steep zig zag path and on the top saw beneath a palm tree

Taylor's elephant fitted with a comfortable howdah—the Elephant knelt and we ascended, waved our hands to our fellow travellers and disappeared into the jungle. The River is now at its lowest point or we could have come up to the village of Rajmahal by water; as it was we were borne along by the Elephant for two or three miles when we entered a large cleared space surrounded by the ruins of a once magnificent palace. In the midst stood two handsome Bungalows, each with a verandah—the outside was white and the pointed reed thatch projecting considerably beyond the walls was supported by white columns, thus forming the verandah. These belonged to Mr Vigors, the District Engineer. The Elephant knelt and I skipped off with alacrity—Taylor, whose vivacity has been subdued by five and twenty Indian summer's suns, descended soberly by means of the ladder carried by the running footman. Mr Vigors was at home and with him two assistant Engineers and a couple of Military officers who had come on a shooting visit. You must remember that this is the centre and most disaffected part of the Southal district and that the officers belonged to a detachment sent to protect the neighbourhood.

Braddon and Glyn, the two Engineers in the house had their tents plundered during last year's riots. Braddon was particularly unfortunate for his cousin visiting him from Calcutta was killed, his jewellery and plate to the amount of £100 was taken and a series of sketches he was preparing for publication were destroyed—his drawings are very clever and indeed he is more of an artist than an Engineer. The Southals are now quiet—in this spot where I write they never entered in force.

Mr Vigors fortified an old Mosque in case of such but it was never required. During the rains in June or July they may band together again for a time, but their leaders are hanged and it is not supposed they will be so mischievous as they were last year.

One month married.

They are simple naked queer looking ruffians and do not look formidable with their spears and bows and arrows—but their numbers are so great that they must not be despised. We want them to work on the Railway but they do not like it and the works flag in consequence.

Well! Mr Vigors received me with kindness—he is an unmarried County Carlow man of about 35. We have a few ideas in common as I know some of his friends, though not many as he has not latterly resided in Ireland. He is very hot-tempered and anxious to start for England in early May—I expect on an interesting errand.

One year married.

We can buy nothing in Rajmahal as there are no shops or markets and there is great difficulty in obtaining servants. I have only three—a *bheestee*, a *mehtur* and a *kitmegar*, as for the present I live with Mr Vigors.

I am looking about for a horse or two and after a time will have I dare say an establishment.

> Give my dear love to Kate and believe me
> Your affectionate Brother Alfred.

A month later, Mr Vigors being on the verge of departure and his farewell parties done with, Alfred found time to write more fully to his mother, from whom he had at last apparently received a backlog of letters.

In the following, some obscure references to relatives of friends at home have been deleted, but there are two points of interest. One concerns Captain George Vaux who is described as commanding craft off the coast of India and having a sister called Elizabeth. There is in our family tree a rather nebulous group of nephews and nieces of Dr Calvert Vaux (Alfred's father) one of whom is shown as 'George Vaux, emigrated to Hindoostan' (no date) who also has a sister Elizabeth and half-sisters Charlotte and Margaret. Brother James also reappears in this letter—apparently also by now become a sailor. He, as already mentioned, is said to have died 'in New Zealand'.

Rajmahal
9 May 1856

My dear Mother,

The last letter I wrote was a bad scrubby kind of epistle—the Bungalow was full of guests who have all departed leaving me alone in a house which is bare of furniture and becoming daily more so as I despatch to each purchaser the goods he bought at Mr Vigors' sale.

Mr Vigors goes to England with the mail that brings this to you but I did not ask him to call on you as his leave is very short and he seemed unwilling to trouble himself about aught but his own affairs. Your letters and scraps enclosed in others give me unfeigned pleasure—your gossip is more graphic than the younger folk's and your motherly solicitude for Em and me, more than all, compensate for the absence of my loved wife and my almost equally loved Mother and sisters.

I see that you have been fretting too much about Emily, I mean Newburgh Emily. None can sympathise more fully in her affliction than I do, but I should be sorry in seeming kindness to induce her to leave a safe and comfortable home with Calvert. Poor John Williams was Calvert's friend; with his success in New York, the light burden of supporting Emily and her infant can not be severely felt—he offers to relieve you and us from anxiety about dear Emily's support. I feel that now our anxiety should be how to arrange a home for our pretty Julia, leaving her elder sister with a prosperous brother and surrounded by kind friends.

It seems ridiculous in me to offer advice when that is the only kind of assistance I can afford—after a time I hope to be able, as I have always considered it my duty and wish, to give more valuable aid.

My income is rather more than I expected, being £500 a year with horse allowance, which more than covers travelling expenses. House rent is paid for me. Eating costs, if we feed as well as we can, £20 a year each—wines are necessary for guests at English prices. Clothing is expensive and may be estimated for comfortable apparel at twice English expenditure. The only heavy item in one's household is Servants. As a married man I should require 25 and each would receive £3, in all £75 a year.

There is some inconvenience and much expense incurred upon settling in a country like this, and believe me it is quite as well for my wife (is she a mother?) that she is not with me. When I have been here longer she may join me with comfort to herself and her presence will afford me unspeakable solace.

I asked you in my last whether you thought my raising one or two hundred pounds would be easily practicable in England and I will tell you why I did so. Most Engineers on arriving in this country obtain an advance of money from the Company. Mr Allan who came out since I did, drew in advance

£100 for the purchase of a horse, and I feel sure that the Company would advance me £200 upon explanation of the purpose to which the sum would be applied.

I have hitherto refrained from this. If I borrowed the money of the Company I should feel bound to repay them as soon as I could, and I should repay £10 per month. I want to use this 8 or 10 pounds a month differently. I think that Julia and you would be a mutual comfort to one another if you resided together, and with that addition to your income you might manage it. When Em leaves London as I trust she will in October I want to leave the money, now payable to her, still payable to Emily Vaux, my mother. Please write to me of this matter, as I shall want to know how to act.

Now there is another matter on which I want your matronly advice.

You know perhaps although I do not, that my wife has borne a son or daughter to me. Rearing children in this country is hazardous and although an infant might be brought here without much disadvantage, yet after 3 or 4 years the climate and habits would weaken its constitution materially. I would forego the pleasure I should feel in seeing my child for its own sake.

Do you not think it might be sent (always supposing that it exists) to some (advertisement):

> 'wife of a clergyman living in a healthy part of the country who with two young children of her own, would be glad, etc. etc . . .'

I have seen such advertisements but really know little about such matters and ask like a dutiful son my mother's opinion.

Rajmahal is not a healthy place for Europeans and we have in the Company's service a resident *Munshi* and also a native Doctor. Good living and caution are necessary. The natives

Servants.

Horses.

are incautious and live irregularly and badly. It is astonishing to see the way they die. They seem to have no spirit or energy to rally against any attack, fever and cholera finding ready victims amongst them.

We have a clear open space in front of the Bungalows beyond which is the jungle. I ought to have game in abundance but I do not keep a *shikaree wallah*, nor do I hunt, so I go without and live upon ducks and fowls. I have given away half a dozen goats and my sheep as I have no shepherd.

Does it not seem strange in Pimlico that I should be obliged to keep a butler, valet, cook and a man to help him, a washerman, a water carrier and a sweep and a groom and a stable understrapper—two doorkeepers and two warriors each with a curved sword, whose duty it is to guard the person of '*Vockus Sahib*'.

I am a small man and I have but one country bred horse and a squirrel to take care of—but I am the greatest man about here so I resign myself. At the same time I must protest that an honest Tipperary 'sarving gal' does more work than all of them together.

I am rather surprised that you should have written so often and never mentioned Elizabeth Vaux and yet her brother has lived here a long time—and I am surprised also that I have forgotten to tell you how stupid I was on one occasion in Calcutta.

Sitting in my room in Spencers Hotel one day before coming up the river, a clean white habited Hindu merchant entered and, after a double salaam, asked me if I was a relative of Captain Vaux who had lived in Calcutta some length of time and was a great friend of his. Mr Thompson was sitting with me and I hastily replied that I had no relatives in Calcutta, upon which the *Baboo* departed without leaving name and address.

I had often been asked if a Rev Fredk Vaux was a relative. He is a government chaplain and I believe no connection of ours—on the instant I thought 'Captain' must belong to the other lot, especially as ours is not a military family and we have no Captain Vauxes. I am now convinced however that he referred to George Vaux who has commanded coastal craft. Since I have been in Rajmahal I have seen his name in the Calcutta directory. I regret that the military title made me dismiss the Hindu too speedily.

Give my love to Charlotte and Margaret.

I am beginning to be anxious about James but think it very probable that he may have changed his ship to one going another voyage. Of course you will let me know of any intelligence you receive of him.

Commend me to those I regard and Believe me
ever your affectionate Son,   Alfred H. Vaux.

When I was a boy in the 1920–30s members of the family were often plagued by enquiries as to our connection with a Colonel Vaux who had apparently been ADC to the Governor of Bombay (or was it Bengal?) for decades on end. None of us had ever heard of him! Perhaps he was a descendant of that George Vaux who 'emigrated to Hindoostan' and settled there. One wonders whether there are any descendants of his in India today.

The above letter rather implies that Alfred had taken over Vigors' job, at least in an acting capacity.

Nothing more is heard of the proposal to farm out the unknown child to some clergyman's family—no doubt the women-folk at home considered the idea to be preposterous. Nevertheless, Alfred's forebodings about the difficulties of rearing children in Bengal in the 1850s were later to prove well founded.

Alfred next amused himself by writing to his sister with a flowery

'Sketch of myself by one of the native Draughtsmen—He left it by chance on the table so I send it to you.'

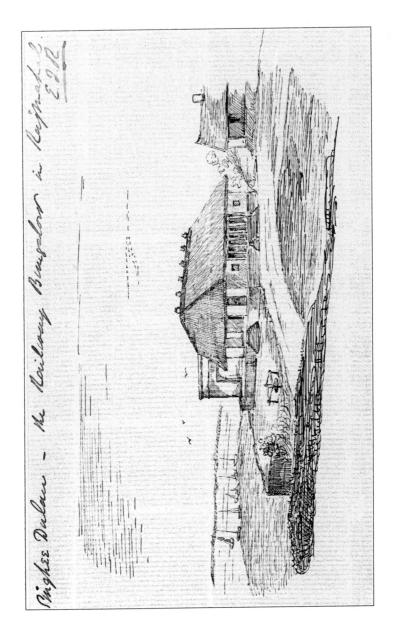

Rajmahal Railway Bungalow.

and poetic description of his bungalow. There were six pages, but a few extracts and some paraphrasing will be enough to include here.

The reference at the end must be to the Crimean War. It was all very well for those in India to be dissatisfied that peace had been concluded—they were not involved with the miseries of the fighting. On the other hand, anything concerning Russian aggression touched them deeply.

Rajmahal

20th May 1856

My dear Julia,

I am lazy and sitting under my office verandah I sketch my abode.

Straight before you, you may notice a grassy sward upon which the office rests—the office you cannot see because it is behind you; beyond the verdant slope a ruddy road leads to a flight of rosy coloured steps—the hue obtained from bricks.

Behind that colonnade are what we call the 'keeping rooms'—cool and protected from the glare. At either end are the two bedrooms, each with a bathroom of which you can see the little windows. The thatch (called *choppa*) is very heavy and provides protection from the scorching sun; arranged along the ridge are water-pots in case of fire. Beyond, the ruins of the old mosque have been skilfully converted into a suite of pretty rooms set amongst ancient domes and pillars.

To the left you may contemplate the river—Holy River Ganger Mai, whose ample stream floats leisurely beyond yon fertile bank. I see the wind is easterly and you can notice shipping. Boats from Dacca bearing cotton, others with frail mast and still more fragile sail carry the produce of our land— in all, maybe a fleet of sixty sail may be seen.

The sun, so bright just now, is overcast; the horizon is obscured—I see a dust-storm is at hand. So come, my Julia, return to the Bungalow. My servants with obsequious attention shall bring from my kitchen (you see the unpretentious shed) a light repast—either some rice and tamarind chutney or perchance you prefer our Indian Fruit, the mango, plantain and a wheaten loaf.

I see the *serai* has been covered with a moist cloth, and placed in the breeze, so we shall be sure of cool water. Water, not brought as you suppose from that well, sunk in ages past for Moslems' need, but from the river carried, boiled and now cooled. The dust is now unpleasant so come and be refreshed.

Wednesday 21 May

I am afraid if you were with me as my fanciful description of my frontispiece supposed, you would not be very comfortable. Rajmahal is in honest truth a somewhat feverish spot. No shops, no church, no roads. Two servants lying sick, and my elephant with sore feet. Three draughtsmen sick in the office and a crowd of work. Dr Fournier applies to me for permission to go down to Calcutta for a month as he must go to conduct a law suit. Don't you think you can make yourself comfortable with mother at home as I proposed in my last?

I hope the rheumatism has left you.

People out here are dissatisfied that peace has been concluded. We do not yet know the terms.

Much pleased to hear from Emily of James writing.

Thank God I have excellent health and spirits.

Ever your affectionate
Brother Alfred.

29 May 56

Dearest Mother,

A line to tell you that I have heard the news of Cal and Emily in the West and am gratified. Old Calvert's success pleases me as much as it does you. He is a brave pushing fellow.

Now I am thinking about Julia and hope you will write to me. If you have not replied to my last please do.

Here we rather expect another outbreak of the Southals during the rains which are just commencing. Do not be anxious about me for this place is out of their country and would be, as it was last year, a refuge for the timid.

Most people here have been sick in fever, but thank God I have had no illness.

Claret, Bitter beer or gin, all diluted, suit me I find better than either plain water or the stronger drinks.

Chicken meat is always sour!

Yr Affectionate Son
Alfred H. Vaux.

We do not actually know what this success of Calvert's was, for he did not win the competition to design Central Park, New York, until April the following year.

Almost immediately after the above letter was written Alfred received splendid news from home. The following pages, dated 2 June, tell it all. (The birth had been on 23 April.)

Rajmahal — 2 M^{rs} —
Engineer preparing to mount puts
out his hand to receive a letter.

announcing the birth of a son.

Ditta retiring to his chamber puts on sleeping costume an on reading the letter,

assumes an attitude of becoming pride.

E. I. Railway

On the banks of the Holy Ganges

Dear Julia,

The Ganges is now seven miles broad at Rajmahal and it forms almost the only means of communication—the only fault is that it flows but one way.

Do not alarm yourself or let Em be anxious about the wild animals here. In the neighbourhood there certainly are Tigeys, and Borking Strictures, and wild boors, and buffy lows and sentry beads and Halley-Gaiters and Copper-umbrella Snakes—all very wenomous and dreadful to talk about but they do no harm, at least I never heard about a Sahib being injured—Mosquitoes and sand flies, insinnivating little creturs are a much greater nuisance. The kites, pariah dogs and jackals frig ones dinner sometimes but they touch no living animal.

Indeed if there were no fever or cholera and if we had but roads, police, churches, a shop nearer than 200 miles, doctors, a little European society and were not obliged to administer and execute the law so often—if we had these little luxuries, the place would not be so bad as it is—and it would not have acquired the name of 'Eden' as it has—you remember Chuzzlewit?

Oh! Julia such thundering big toads, upon my credit, as big as a warming pan—and the little chaps get into your boots, and you feel them crunch as you pull them on—off comes the foot gear and out jumps a and scuttles away.

You would not mind these things after a little time—they make capital stock for a letter and elicit I hope a great deal of Pimlico commiseration—but they are nothing at all in practice believe me.

I shall answer your nice letter on your return from Manchester soon—till then and ever believe me your affect Brother

Alfred.

Rajmahal,
East Indian Railway
18 August 1856

My dearest Mother,

Your letter of the 9th July with my Em's and Julia's scrap has just come to hand. But why, my much respected and dear parent, why did you cross your writing? Your hand was firm and ideas ran fluently on to the paper whilst you were inditing the epistle, and believe me that the letter was valuable enough to deserve a larger sheet. As it was the ink was so thick, there were so many lines and the words were so boldly formed that they proved almost illegible. Half an hour was all the time I could have to read the letters and reply. It was insufficient so there is a great chance that this will miss the homeward bound steamer. The country is so deeply inundated that postal communication is now rather uncertain. The other evening I was coming home on the Elephant, and after swimming some distance along the Mail road, I had to make the Elephant clamber up the bank to avoid a fishing-net stretched from one side of the road to the other!

Your letter when read was very interesting, the worst part was when you mentioned Emily's fever, but that I hope has subsided, and you are now all in good health. I deeply feel all your kindness to my wife and I hope you will very seriously take her to task for not being careful of herself.

On her passage out she will in that matter have to trust to herself and no [sic] friends with kind solicitude to attend to her. The journey is a pleasure trip in October if you will but think it so. I wrote yesterday a letter to Emily with one for you. There is ample money in hand for all her expenses—perhaps you will have to wait a little time for it to be paid—but when you have it, do not think of making things for her. An

Indian outfitting shop is worse still—the best plan is to hire a fly or a cab and to drive to the best shops and buy what is wanted. Probably Mr Noad or his clerks in Alderman's Walk will see after the passage and provide a ticket for her, so that really if you all take things quietly you will have very little trouble.

My dear sisters' plan will I dare say be a very nice one, and I hope for all success to their little school in Croydon. I was at first rather opposed to Emily's return from America as I thought that anxiety for you would be the result—but you all know your own affairs best. If my wife can spare any thing out of her little outfit sum, I should like her to make Emily a present, but perhaps that had better be deferred for a time. I have great financial hopes from the scholars—but mind that you do not mix yourself up in the matter.

With dutiful love, your affectionate Son

Alfred H. Vaux

Tell Em before she goes to Mr Noad, that she must be able to say exactly by which steamer she can be ready for. There is no occasion to hurry herself too much, but she must say what she means. You all think that the preparation is a formidable affair, but you know that the fact is:

<u>A days shopping and a cab for Waterloo station next morning</u>!

It would appear from this that the widowed Emily is now on her way from the USA and is going into partnership with her sister, or sisters, to run a small school.

Alfred's letters were more frequent as the time drew near for his wife to sail for India and he became more than ever convinced that the womenfolk would somehow make a mess of things, so that Em would miss the boat. Certainly they were all up to their eyes, with mother moving house to Canterbury Road in Croydon, where they had all lived before, Emily and her baby Cuthbert returning from the USA and preparations to be made for the little school to be set up. One suspects that, meanwhile, Em was calmly preparing to move herself and her six-month-old son half across the world. There is no evidence that she ever complained or revealed any apprehension.

So far the name of the little boy had not cropped up in letters. We know that he had in fact been christened Alfred Robert Brickwood Vaux. Confusingly, his parents referred to him as 'Brickwood', his brothers were to call him 'Bob' and my generation knew him as 'old Uncle Alfred' (he lived to be ninety-two).

On 2 Sept 1856 Alfred wrote again to his mother; he seemed to feel that things were getting out of hand:

> I do not know where you may be so I address a note to the care of Uncle E.C.B. just to express a hope that when you receive it all anxiety on the score of my wife will have been diminished by her having been fairly shipped off with a label round her neck consigned to me. I know your loving sympathy will have aided her in many ways but your three daughters will have given you enough employment for your active mind. Perhaps Mr Noad did not give the money at the right time, many things may have interrupted the harmony of the course I proposed but I quite hope that Em will start on the 20th October.

He then appears to get cold feet and, after reference to the uncertainty of life in India, expresses doubts that—despite being 'in tolerable health'—he will live to see Em's arrival. He explains that in India a good system exists for helping those suddenly widowed and gives details of his bank account and insurance policy. He has ensured that the Railway Company will arrange a passage home for his wife and child and hopes that there will also be a small pension. He puts his trust in God. Having thoroughly depressed everyone, he encloses a 'scrap' to greet his sister on her return from the USA and hopes that the two Emilies will be able to meet. But he soon cheers up.

E.I.R. Rajmahal
17th October 1856

My dear Mother,

I suppose that I may regularly now expect letters from Croydon. I like to think of you in the old town again and think that you might be very happy there if dear Emily and Julia are with you. Canterbury Road is a nice place, is it not? Does the same postman bring your letters? We have no double knocks in the morning here, no bells rung by impatient letter carriers.

Our little town has though been busy for the last week—a few days ago the Commander in Chief and his staff sailed up the river; one of his aide de camps called upon me—on the same day the Lord Chief Justice, Sir James Colville, walked up from his steamer to Singhee Dalau [the Railway Bungalow] and I had to attend to him. While he was here a little quiet joke occurred. Some of our people had quite illegally imprisoned a boatman. He somehow or other escaped and while the Chief Justice was sitting with me, came up to the steps and putting his hands together began a long statement. I stopped him and, though I did not understand the case thoroughly, explained that he was a poor man who had been wrecked lately, so Sir James gave him a rupee and the man walked off to the river.

We have now the Commissioner of the Southal Pergumahs here and another magistrate who have a great deal of business to get through—since last year's outbreak a commissioner has been appointed and some of the rebels are to be tried.

Mr Gale, the Commissioner, is a very great sportsman, or
rather was when he was a younger man. In India every man
is judged by his salary—so Mr Gale is a very great man, as he
receives £300 every month. He dined with me the other
evening and the next day I had to send the chairs over to his
tent for a 'deputation' and a Bible to swear his witnesses upon.

I expect that I shall have to appear before him to-day as a
criminal. A man selling cloth from the Bazaar cheated me this
morning, so I ordered my porter to drive and beat him out of
my grounds. It was not right I suppose, indeed I am sure it was
not, but it is almost impossible to avoid violence in this country.
No native by any chance at any time deals with you in such a
way that you can suspect him of honesty. His roguery is manifold.

The river is falling now and the malaria from flooded land
is rising. One third of my people are sick. The native habit of
throwing corpses into the river is bad also. Sometimes a des-
perate effluvium arises and I know that a body has been washed
ashore near me. To-day as I walked on the river bank close to
my bungalow, I noticed a skeleton which was not there yesterday. Jackals had dragged it from the river and consumed the flesh
in that short time—I heard the divils at work in the night.

We are a strange people out here and not agreeable in our
habits at all times. Everything you know is difficult to procure
but I have a little furniture now ready for Em when she
appears.

I do not expect to be able to reach Calcutta to meet her as
I do not know when she starts, and it would be too great a
loss of time to go down and return with her. However, I hope
to be able to make arrangements for her comfort. Landing in
Calcutta and a residence of the first week in India will be
odious I know. If someone meets her it will be so much easier
and she will have what money she requires.

I write by this post to Aden expecting that she will be there on 14 November [she got there 13 December], but it is all surmise and I do not yet know if she has received the requisite money—many things may prevent her starting on the 20th October.

Your account of Julia being in good health pleases me. I dare say Emily is now in Surrey and her bold little boy. What is his name—I mean how do you call him?

Now mind my dear Mother that when my wife has left England you must write to me—I will send the postage stamps. Recollect I know Croydon and it won't do to tell me that there is nothing to write about. One of our Inspectors, Mr Adams, was an overseer during the sewage disturbance which you recollect in Croydon, so you see we know all about you.

I mean to write regularly. Give my love to the dear girls.

Believe me your affectionate Son
Alfred H. Vaux.

Rajmahal
Tuesday 16th Dec 1856

My dear Julia,

You see by my little enclosure that you have not lost all your old admirers and that the attractions which now charm Croydon are well remembered in Bengal. The 70th Native Infantry were passing down the river yesterday from Delhi and encamped near my bungalow, so I called on Phillip Harris who is adjutant of his regiment and appears a gentlemanly handsome man. I was asked to the mess but declined. His father is senior captain of the 70th and has staff employment as Colonel of Gwalior Contingent Corps so I did not see him.

I liked to hear in your letter of the cows grazing near the house and the large trees in the grounds of the gentleman opposite, but I do not pity you your long walk to teach the wee children at all—indeed I should like it myself.

I have no news but that the weather is delightful—English clothing and blankets—if I had a fireplace I would like artificial heat. The country is not however yet healthy. When Mr Vigors left, our population of Europeans was about 30—six have died since of different complaints, one every month. I am told I read the burial service <u>beautiful</u> but wish I had not the practice. Nightly I give thanks for the many mercies I receive and pray for their continuance on myself and family. You and the dear little circle are believe me never forgotten.

I was struck by an affecting incident the other day which I suppose no one but myself noticed. Richard Adams, one of our rough hardy inspectors who had no ailment during his two years residence here was seized with cholera and narrowly escaped death. His wife and four children were in fever, so were his servants. After much suffering he recovered somewhat and was able to walk about—at this juncture his youngest child died in its mother's arms. The poor man had to make the coffin for his favourite son's remains and next day rode in to me to bury it in the cleared part of the jungle.

I was much touched when I saw the simple solemn little cavalcade arrive in the evening and thought of his previous night's work, so dreary for a sick man. These serious topics force themselves occasionally on my mind and are not unsalutary, but you must not think I am down hearted, for I am in good health and am enjoying life very much, anticipating with pleasure the arrival of my baggage and the additional inconvenience shipped per *Pera* on the 20th of last month.

I have made arrangements for starting on Monday next for Calcutta and hope I shall not be thwarted. I intend travelling night and day *palkee dawk* that is in a palanquin borne by natives. The country through which I pass has plenty of wild boars, wolves, tigers and bears so I hope to give a thrilling account in my next of a terrific conflict:

Scene   – jungle
Time   – midnight
Actors   – leopard, self and serpents
Spectators   – jackals and timid coolies
<u>All by the light of the moon</u>

Adventures or not, I shall be sure to write again soon to you for loving my boy as you write that you do.

With best love to yourself
Yr affectionate Brother
Alfred H. Vaux.

Calcutta
30th Decr 1856

My dear Mother,

I am wishing you and dear Julia Em and Cuthbert a happy New Year while I wait with some trepidation for the arrival of wife & boy. I spent Christmas Day in a palanquin and thought much of my much loved mother in her Croydon house. I hope Emily will bring me good tidings of Kate.

6 January 57—

all safe and my darling boy twice as big and bright a fellow as I expected—dear little son how thankful I am to my God for the protection he has afforded to my wife and my boy—and you too my loved mother daily do I think of your kind solicitude—lately again sorely tried during Kate's confinement.

Bless her dear heart how I have thought of her—Em brings me news of the birth of a girl—of course I wish to see her and the intelligent good Cuthbert. I think you ought to be

Calcutta
30ᵗ Decʳ. 1856 -

My dear Mother,
    I am wishing you and dear
Julia Eve and Cuthbert a happy
new year while I wait with some
anxiety for the arrival of wife & boy.
I spent Christmas day in a palanquin
and thought much of my much
loved mother in her Croydon home.
I hope Emily will bring me good
tidings of Kate —

6. January 57 —
all safe and my darling
boy twice as big and bright
a fellow as I expected — dear
little son how thankful
I am to my God for the
protection he has afforded
to my wife and my
boy — and you too my
loved mother daily do
I think of your kind
solicitude — lately again
severely tried during
Kate's confinement

Letter to Mother.

53

very happy and contented my mother—! Funds are scarce with us all but very little money will provide for our real wants.

You have been a very useful affectionate parent to us and I always think that we do not deserve half your kindness. You know that you have our love and from none do you receive more than from your dutiful son

Alfred H. Vaux.

In the last line above is the first mention of Catherine's confinement—presumably her first—which gives a clue to the date of her marriage to Robert Withers. Further on in this letter Alfred mentions that Em has just told him that Kate has had a daughter—who was, incidentally, the first of her nine children.

4

EMILY

One needs a cool head when referring to any connection of Alfred
Vaux named Emily. To list them:

Alfred's mother was Emily, née Brickwood

His elder sister was Emily, who married John Williams

His first wife was Emily, sister of John Williams

Emily and John Williams' father was, like Alfred's, a City of
London doctor and the children of both families were very close.
Dr Williams died before his daughter's wedding and the family
home seems to have broken up, John going off with his wife,
Alfred's sister, to the United States. It seems that after their
marriage Alfred's wife lived with his mother and sisters. The Vaux
family, close and devoted to one another, drew young Emily (Em
to all) into their circle, the elder Mrs Vaux, now in her sixties,
being adored by everyone. Later, Emily writes to the old lady as
'Mother' and signs off to the girls as 'your sister'. Occasionally she
encloses a note to her own mother 'who has moved, I suppose,
but I am ignorant of her new abode'.

As the crow flies, Rajmahal is about ninety-five miles from
Calcutta, but we know that it took ten days by paddle steamer on
the winding Ganges and Hooghly rivers. It was probably about
two hundred miles by the jungle 'Mail Road' along which Alfred's
palanquin sped 'night and day', the bearers changing over at the

rest houses at each stage. Indeed, he once mentions that there was no shop nearer than two hundred miles.

While Alfred spent his Christmas Day in the swaying palanquin, his beloved Em was about to leave Ceylon and enter the Bay of Bengal on the last lap of her journey to Calcutta. The experience had been anything but the 'pleasure trip' promised by Alfred for, apart from the rigours of crossing the desert from Alexandria to Suez, she had been ill throughout the two sea voyages. With a small baby to care for, the eleven-week journey, from 20 October to 5 January, must have been a nightmare.

If she wrote from Malta or Egypt these letters have not survived, for the first we have is from Aden, though posted in Ceylon. In this she refers to the baby (Alfred Robert Brickwood Vaux) as 'Alley', but her husband was soon to put a stop to this indignity, and the boy was thereafter known as 'Brickwood'.

Ship *Bentinck*

Aden December 13th 1856

My dear Julia,

We have just arrived at Aden and while we are at anchor I will try and write a few lines. You must all forgive me for my last shabby scrap, but could you have seen how I have suffered I believe I should not need to ask your clemency—as long as the ship is moving I am ill!! Dearest Alley is very bright and well and keeps his flesh [*sic*] wonderfully. I always strive to attend to his wants somehow or another—it does seem strange that in a ship where there are nearly 200 hands employed no one can take my boy for a few minutes.

December 23rd I was taken ill again while writing the above and I could not finish it at Aden. Most thankfully can I say that I am a trifle better. The Dr of the ship has me under his care. I take tonics 4 times a day and plenty of wine and porter.

Mrs Emily Eliza Vaux (née Williams) ('Em') (1828–1865),
Alfred's first wife.

He wishes me to wean Alley [b.23/4/56, now 35 weeks] but
I find it impossible to do so by myself.

We expect to be at Ceylon tomorrow night and at Calcutta
about the 4th Jan—how I look for the day!! My spirit has
nearly failed me several times during the heat—at 100 degrees
in the shade! Dearest Baby keeps well and grows fat and healthy
looking, indeed he is the wonder of the ship! A life on board
these ships is not to be envied I can assure you. But when I
am with my dear and my head feels a little clearer I hope to
be able to write many amusing pages. I lose much of the usual
chit chat through not being able to join the Table—but my
eyes keep open for all that. Dearest Julia, how I should think

of you all on Christmas Day! I wonder will Kate and her little Miss Withers dine with you! Mind you tell me everything. Am I missed? I miss all the dear old faces round me sadly and when I have been so ill I have felt the loss of my Mother's [in-law] gentle kindly manner. Dr Maitland says he never knew such madness as my coming out alone without help—too much for any woman. So I thank God for the strength that has carried me this far—and pray that I may yet reach Calcutta. My little darling thriving so well helps me cope.

I have had two letters from dear Alf—in the last he says that he does not think that he can meet me, oh I trust he will. The food is horrid here and nothing really fit to eat, all the passengers up in arms about it. You must look out in *The Times*, for many declare they will write and expose the Company.

The weather is clear and lovely but piping. Just fancy dear Alley with beads of perspiration all over his arms and hands—as to me I sit as it were in a bath. Dear Alf will find his wife much shrunk for my dresses hang quite loose over me—indeed to tell the truth my vanity is quite disturbed at going to meet him as such a Scare Crow.

December 25th. 6 o'clock a.m. I was very ill all yesterday and am going ashore with Capt and Mrs Battey. The Dr says it will do me good so I think I may venture on that plea to disobey dear Alf's wishes. We are to have a ride and then return to the ship to dinner—of course I take little Alley with me and young Mrs Makecross has proved a kind friend to me, always on the alert to help when there is such need when carrying the Boy. I know your thoughts will be with us to-day—tell everyone they are remembered . . . Good bye dear all . . . God bless you my dears . . .

Here 'dear Alley' begins to tug at the paper, on which the tearstains are still visible, and the letter ends rather incoherently.

The next letter is written from Calcutta to her mother-in-law—by now Em is a changed girl.

Deans Hotel,

Howrah. Jany 5th

My dear Mother,

At last my long journey is over and I am once more in my dear husband's presence. The *Bentinck* arrived at Calcutta on the 2nd about ½ past 5 p.m. I had received a letter at Khadjuree [Calcutta Signal Station] that morning to say Alf would come to meet me so you may imagine my state of anxiety when we really cast anchor. Julia insisted on my giving a full and particular account of our meeting, but all I can tell is I was waiting in the Ladies room, just in the act of nursing the Boy, when I heard the old voice at the door say 'Where are you, Em?' I gave Alley to the Stewardess and went to meet my dearest. Afterwards I presented him to Father who was much impressed at 'such a big boy'. Tell Emily Alley wore on the occasion one of her pretty frocks with the special trimming and a Leghorn hat and feathers and little shoes and stockings!! I think Papa was very pleased with the first impression.

Calcutta being quite full Alf had taken rooms at Deans Hotel, Howrah—the other side of the river—where we lost no time in getting to. My small leather bag was all the luggage we took that evening, so that only a few minutes elapsed between our meeting and leaving the ship. It was very curious to see dear Papa take the boy in his arms while I got in and out of the boat. But when we reached the hotel I found he had engaged an Ayah who was waiting to take care of young Master—it is rather awkward considering that I cannot understand one word she says—or she mine—but it makes me alert in learning Bengali! It has been no easy matter, I assure you, to give my boy into her keeping and let her do all for him. He has been very cross and fretful but this morning a little rash made its appearance so perhaps that accounts for it.

Poor Papa has had full experience of the sleepless nights we parents are subjected to, for these nights Alley has teased me sadly and of course given his father a dose! All this time I have not told you how your dear son looks. I think pretty well— his face somewhat thinner and longer looking and perhaps a little older and more thoughtful, yet I can hardly bring myself to believe that we have been separated for one whole year.

Jany 6th. My letter must be written piece meal, I find, for when dear Alf comes in good bye to pens, ink and paper.

To-day I have been over to Calcutta—first to call on Mrs Battey (a fellow passenger) then with her to the Exchange to make some purchases. Alf had a carriage and pair for the day. After spending a goodly number of rupees for house and Baby we had an hour's drive on the 'Course', the Rotten Row of Calcutta. If my time were not limited I could tell you many queer things but for this letter I must restrain myself. Tomorrow I go with Baby and Ayah to Tiffin with Mrs Battey and on Thursday we leave Howrah for Home, ten days' journey by steamer.

We are very anxious to hear of Kate and look forward to your first letter. I must again trouble you to send the enclosed to my Mother as I do not know her abode.

The rest of this letter is missing, but she must have been very near the end of it. Luckily, Alfred takes up the tale four weeks later, the following being rather abridged editorially.

Rajmahal

2 February 1857

My dear Kate,

It seems an age since I wrote to you. Have I congratulated you on the birth of my dear little niece? Em gave me a nice description of your pretty Catherine and I was delighted to hear all about you and the infant. Now Kate do write a description of your wee child for I am beginning to know almost as much about babies as the veriest matron of you all. I am quite a family man now having been very frequently and severely moistened and have had my night's rest broken often. On some occasion when you are sitting quietly with your husband tell him how much pity he meets with from a brother in like distress. Tell Robert I often allow my thoughts to fly over to Winchester Hurst, when at night in airy costume I vainly endeavour to pacify Master Brickwood and strive to still his roar which loudly is heard above the cry of the jackals and other disturbances of the night.

I am gradually obtaining furniture for our bungalow, already tables and chairs have been purchased and of course they cost a great deal of money. Emily is not used to strangers coming in and locating themselves with us and I do not think you would like it at first. I have orders to build a 'Guest Room' here and to furnish it at the Railway Company's expense and perhaps that may when finished take some of our strangers.

Our Railway works are going on again as the contractor has been discharged and we, the Engineers, have to supervise the construction of the line ourselves—it is a most laborious disagreeable duty and ought to be highly paid. After a time I hope that our increased work will bring an increase in emolument.

I made a hard fight before going down to Calcutta endeavouring to be removed from Rajmahal but did not succeed.

The authorities have difficulty in procuring men who will live here and indeed it is not easy to find those who can live here for it is as unhealthy a location as any in India. However, upon the whole I am very thankful to say that I have had as good health here as in Ireland and Emily seems well satisfied and the boy thrives.

What do you think of the new house at Croydon? I should think it is more comfortable than the old one and that Emily, Julia and Mother will be happy there with young Cuthbert [Emily's son] to prevent them becoming too sedate and quiet.

Kiss the little Catherine for me, my first niece,

Give my regards to Robert and believe me

Your affectionate Brother

Alfred H. Vaux.

After she had been there about a month, Em wrote her first letter from Rajmahal. It was addressed to Alfred's other sister.

Rajmahal Feb 28th

(Finished 2 March 1857)

My dear Julia,

In the hope that this epistle may reach you in time, first and foremost many Happy Returns, dearest. Tell our dear Emily to be very lively and jocose on this occasion to make up for this Emily V's non-appearance. In my mind's eye I can see you all—perhaps in some few years we may meet on this day to 'compare notes' and judge how old Time has used us. Alfred says that I am so much altered from what I was when we were married that he does not think people would know me at all. If such be the case in two years I wonder what a few more and an Indian climate will do for one. Yet I have seen many ladies who have lived years in this country and look quite young and pretty still.

Last Sunday, while we were reading Service together, a 'Sahib' called with letters of introduction to beg our hospitality for a few days—only himself, wife, 4 children and two other gentlemen?!! Making in all 8 persons. Well, my dear, about 4 o'clock the steamer landed these said persons, lady and children more vivid in colour than the brightest parrot. We managed to shake 6 of them down and sent the two Sahibs over to the Office Bungalow. They stayed till Wednesday and to tell you the truth I was pleased at their departure. Three young children dirty and dressed in tawdry finery plus the youngest only 16 months old, a fine boy but being very poorly, crying and fretting the whole day. No Ayah and the Mother too inert even to comb their hair which hung about like old matting! I felt quite shocked at their appearance and only pray I may never become so lost to all sense of neatness and industry as to let my boy follow in the train of such poor neglected children. Our chief difficulty was to obtain food enough—our cook seems to have a dislike to put too much on the Table—or perhaps it is we consume so very little ourselves that he supposes all white folk eat in the same proportion.

We have all been poorly this week. Poor Papa sore throat and attacks of fever, Baby a dreadful cold and myself bad sore throat and mouth, though better to-day. Papa looks himself again but feels weak. This fever is indeed a fearful thing! Last night a Mrs and Mr Mellor called on us. They had come down from Pierre Pointe in a little boat and landed here to await the steamer, which was expected, to take them on to Calcutta. Mr Mellor (quite a young man) has been suffering much from fever and looks all skin and bone. They are going down for a change. His wife, such a sweet little creature, been married 18 months, looks the picture of health and happiness—she only came out here ('on spec' Alf says) two years since. They used

Emily's writing was not always easy to decipher.

to live in the 'Begum's Tomb' near here but have gone 15 miles up country.

I have made my debut on elephant-back and had two nice long rides. I rather like it only it seems strange to be mounted so high, about 7 feet with the howdah; some elephants stand 8 feet though. The poor thing died last week, she caught cold, a large swelling came in the neck and she choked. The ground about here was too hard to dig a grave for her, so she was cut up and thrown into the river for the fishes! We get plenty of fish but I cannot say I fancy it although I often have to eat it. The Prawns are particularly fine, but thank you NO! Not for me! Do you remember Alf's story about the Eels? A second instalment might be told here.

I have been out here two months this very day and to tell the truth am not yet tired of my husband!! A fact!

I think the House looks rather more comfortable than when I arrived—but I am sadly put out, for the dust is so intolerable that it is useless to keep pretty things on one's table. Books obstinately turn their corners up in your very face and flowers fade in about 4 hours. Dust—Dust—Dust!!! My saucy husband is sitting in the easy chair reading a novel called *Time the Avenger* and has just quoted a passage (much to his enjoyment): 'In women, the inclination for meddling is often stronger than the fear of being thought impertinent.' What think you! I have picked a few very pretty wild flowers and intend to try and dry them for your inspection, but do not be disappointed should they never reach you—they are so tender that I fear I shall not succeed.

Did I tell you that what things I brought out do very nicely—only had I taken all light Boots it would have been better. I want a thick dress and more flannels—Bonnets I might as well have omitted. I never wear them. Alf bought me a pretty grey felt hat which I trimmed with 4 rows of black velvet and a couple of grey tassels. The blue dress you liked so much was quite spoilt crossing the desert. Baby took all the colour out [*sic*]. My black silk too was quite done for, having to be nurse and everything else aboard the river steamer did for it. With the exception of a riding habit I think I managed pretty well in my purchases. Many thanks dear for your kind offer of sending out things—some day I hope to avail myself.

Mr Vigors (do you remember the name?) is expected out by the next mail—he brings a wife and wants to come back here. I shall be very sorry if we are obliged to turn out for I like the Bungalow, and I know the idea annoys dear Alf much—most likely my next letter will tell you. Dear Papa is better of his attacks but is weak and I have made him take a little quinine. Mother's scales are <u>so</u> useful.

There now follows much technical talk about babies, Em comparing her own with Kate's 'new Miss Withers', and going into the whole question of teething. 'Dear Alf' has had his sleep so disturbed that he cannot work by day, so has moved into a room at the far end of the bungalow, leaving Em and the baby at the other. All this is so heavily cross-written as to be almost unreadable.

Ask Kate how she would like Robert to choose <u>the Back</u> Kitchen for his apartment!! Our Ayah sleeps in my room now but I cannot say she helps me in the least.

With special love and good wishes, ever your
Affect sister Emily V.

<u>PS</u> - My dear a <u>French couple</u> have made their appearance at the house since I finished this epistle! The lady cannot speak a word of English or Bengali and <u>neither</u> of us can speak French! They are to remain <u>a few days</u>!! I feel at my wits end—it is bad enough that <u>all</u> one's servants do not understand

a single word of one's mother tongue! How you would laugh to hear me talking, <u>or rather acting</u>. <u>March 2nd.</u>

The next is the last cheerful letter we are to see from Em for a long time to come. She has not yet, incidentally, revealed to those at home that she is now pregnant.

Rajmahal, June 4th 1857

My dearest Julia,

Your letters are such a comfort to me, indeed I may say <u>us</u> for Papa delights in them just as much as I do. Your description of Cuthbert's 'Milk maw' made Alf shake with laughter—the dear little fellow, how I long to see him. Little Brickwood grows so strong and so dearly loves his <u>whip</u> that Papa says he must be destined to be a Coachman or an Ostler. Papa dotes on him <u>except when he cries.</u>

The weather is still <u>very</u> hot, last night was something dreadful, so we both feel weak and <u>stewed like</u> to-day. The rash over my body does not get any better I am sorry to say, and it worries me.

The Insects still abound. What do you think? A few days since I found the locks of my two Wardrobes in a strange state—I had great difficulty in getting in the Keys and when I did succeed could not turn them. Of course I imagined some of the servants must have been meddling with them. After poking about some time out came some sticky stuff and after a little further trouble I managed to open the drawers. I told Alf of this but he could not make it out, however the mystery was soon solved. I actually saw <u>The Bees</u> go in at the key hole and I find that in three locks there are Bee Hives! I must get them taken off and cleaned and always stuff paper in the locks until the Bees are gone.

June 14th. Mr and Mrs Vigors are away and I do not suppose they will return until we have taken up our abode in the Office Bungalow. Some little alterations have had to be made and the work people are still there or we would have removed long ere this. The new Bungalow is progressing and when finished will be a delightful place, far better than this. Dear Alf is taking so much pains about it—every evening we go together to see how all goes on and he tells me to suggest what I would like done. By and by we will send a sketch of it, as it is to be.

We have not been very easy these last few days as there are rumours of another Southal outbreak. However, it seems it was but talk.

The letter ends here, on 14 June 1857, and we do not know whether the next page was lost or never written. There is irony in the last sentence, for there does not seem to have been any trouble with the Southals. But Em did not know that, only ten days earlier, the Sepoys in Cawnpore—further up the Ganges—had revolted and the little British community there, which included about two hundred women and children, was already surrounded and isolated. The Indian Mutiny had begun.

5

THE INDIAN MUTINY

Although apparently unknown to Rajmahal, the Indian Mutiny had begun on Sunday 10 May 1857 at Meerut. The following day Delhi also fell into the hands of rebels. It should be remembered that at that time the Company's Indian Army numbered 311,000, while in the whole of India there were no more than 40,000 British troops, who thus faced odds of about eight to one. Although in fact a few of the native regiments and numerous individuals remained loyal (especially in Bombay and Madras), and a small number of British troops was available from the Persian Gulf while others were intercepted on their way to China, it was not really for a year that adequate reinforcements arrived from Britain. In the meantime there was ferocious fighting, with the British always outnumbered though often successful, during which the Mutineers committed a series of appalling massacres of British women and children. Prominent in the latter activity was the local ruler in Cawnpore, one Nana Sahib, who had assumed control of the rebellious troops in Oudh.

A fortnight after Emily's letter to Julia, the last in the previous chapter, Alfred wrote to his mother:

Rajmahal

28 June 1857

My dear Mother,

How anxious you must be about us and with what just cause! Every mouth is filled with talk about the state of affairs and daily we hear the most dreadful accounts of our acquaintances being killed in the horrible massacres you have read of.

Bhagulpore about seventy miles from us on one side [i.e. north-west] and Murshidabad about the same distance on the other [i.e. south-east towards Calcutta] are both in an unsettled state. Native regiments occupy them and though they are not in mutiny no reliance can be placed upon their good faith. At Bhagulpor, or rather on the other side of the Southal country, poor Mr Norman Leslie was killed as he sat after dinner in his verandah. Three men of his own cavalry cut his body in two. The act did not meet the approbation of their companions who held a drum-head court martial on the delinquents, placed each on an elephant, led them to three trees and hanged them. The villains singing 'Allah Hu!' as the elephants were driven from beneath them.

While I was absent on the twenty-fifth an alarm came in from above, the Commissioner of the District forcibly recommended every female in the place to leave it for Calcutta in the Steamer then at the *Ghat*, so my poor wife packed up a few clothes and when I returned she was ready to start with our dear boy. In an hour afterwards they went on board a barge towed behind the Steamer and there they are now on route to Calcutta, huddled together with sixty children and a score or so more ladies on the deck, travelling a voyage of ten days in the most inclement season of India—mid-Summer and the rains unusually delayed and now commencing.

They must be in a bad plight poor creatures—may God help them! When all shall mend is impossible to foretell—much depends on what is done at Delhi now held by the rebels. It is reported that the place has fallen with great loss but though the news is probable we cannot rely on it. I think that Rajmahal is as far as circumstances allow safe for the present. Within a few miles are thirty Railway men who might be gathered on short notice and the river behind us gives a good chance of retreat.

God bless you my dear Mother
Your affect. Son Alfred H. Vaux.

In fact, Delhi was not recaptured until 20 September. However, on the very day—25 June—that poor Em and Brickwood embarked on that agonising voyage down to Calcutta, the series of events began in Cawnpore which was to lead so swiftly to the most gruesome massacre of the whole insurrection.

Rajmahal 25 July 1857

My dear Mother,

It is with a sad heart that I write to you, for I have had bad accounts of both wife and child. They are in a respectable lodging house in Calcutta in the best locality but the room Em has is very hot and she needs fresher and purer air. Brickwood Baby is suffering from his teeth, the four eye teeth coming through at once. He seems to have had and indeed not recovered from a very bad attack of dysentery and nausea and all tell me the child is quite changed, always quiet, weak and languid and scarcely to be recognised for the fine child he was here.

Dr Collins, who was for a time in Rajmahal and who obtained a better appointment in Calcutta, attends them and writes me a bulletin every day, but the post now takes three days so a week passes before an answer is received to a letter. Emily was subjected to so much hardship aboard that miserable flat behind the Steamer, and so much anxiety since, that a miscarriage is the result. Dr Collins writes that he can hardly tell if it has yet taken place but that it promises to be lingering.

71

Emmie is not allowed to rise from her bed and of course cannot write to me. In a letter I received from Mrs Vigors this morning she says that my wife is so weak that unless a change for the better occurs she thinks she must sink. I will give another report by the 'Southampton' Mail.

Perhaps you see a paper regularly now that such bad news arrives every mail from India and by the press you learn many of the occurrences around us which must shock all civilised beings. The latest news from the North West is that General Havelock assaulted Cawnpore which was in the hands of Nana Sahib, defeated him after an hour and a half fighting and retook the place. This ruffian had regularly besieged Sir Hugh Wheeler who with a gallant little band had fortified the place. It was not until weeks of privation, their food and ammunition gone and the leader slain, that the small body of soldiers surrendered. They were immediately slaughtered and Nana Sahib took possession of the town in triumph. Some time necessarily elapsed before a sufficiently large force could be sent against him and when General Havelock reached Cawnpore and Nana found he could do no more, he blew up the magazine, killed all our women and children and retreated to Bhitoor. Havelock could not waste time in following him as he was to proceed immediately to succour the inhabitants of Lucknow, where Sir Henry Lawrence has just been killed. Our men behaved very well as usual but were scarce to be controlled—can you imagine how Englishmen's blood would boil when they saw, on the line of march, such things as children's shoes lying by the road, with the feet in them?

Part of the China Expedition has passed up the Ganges: a detachment of the 5th Fusiliers were in Rajmahal on Sunday and the officers gave me a call. They were in high spirits and all in good health, scarcely yet understanding the change in their destination, anticipating Shanghai and going to Delhi! They are brave fellows and we want more like them. The *Himalaya* has just arrived in the Calcutta river with 900 and there are more to follow before that army comes which we must have from England.

We expect a rise of the Mussulman population on 3rd August, the Mahommedan festival, but I hope that though not killed that snake is scotched. We must not dream of safety in India until these mutinous sepoys are disarmed and our European army as a permanence doubled.

One of our Railway Inspectors on Monday night found three people inside his bungalow removing his furniture. He sprang out of bed and shot one dead and was running from the house to attack the rest when his drawers became loose and falling to his knees so hampered him that they escaped!

Two Southals have been hanged for a murder two years ago, so I think the bad spirits have had a lesson sufficient for one week. All the decent people here would lose by any disturbances and they know it, so we need not fear them. What we must dread are the scamps who alone are in sufficient numbers to eat us without our flavouring their curry.

I write not of any of you dear ones, but my heart is with you and you are in my thoughts daily. God bless you my Mother and you all

> Your Affect Son
> Alfred H. Vaux.

Alfred is very nearly right in his account of events at Cawnpore—except that they were even worse than he thought. The whole episode had been one of treachery by Nana Sahib, who twice broke his word. The women and children he slaughtered numbered over two hundred. The exact number was never known, most of their bodies being thrown down a well from which they could not be recovered.

It seems that after writing the above, Alfred can have lost no time in getting down to Calcutta. Perhaps, even, he was sent for, for he could not have left his post without permission. There seems to be a letter missing before the following.

On board the *Helen*
18 August 1857

My dear Mother,

I shall send this via Marseilles as I know that you are anxious about us and our boy. Really we have improved much in health since I wrote last. Emily is better though very weak and nervous and Brickwood is no more a healthy child. We remained with Mr and Mrs Turnbull till last Saturday and they were very kind. They had no other guests and were much more attentive and considerate than I could have hoped and I am grateful to them. Calcutta is now so crowded with refugees from the upper provinces that lodging of any kind is difficult to obtain. This made our residence in the most pleasant part of Calcutta a greater boon. There is always a cool breeze at night and the daily drive on the Course refreshed Emily.

I have now hired a couple of boats for a fortnight and we are cruising on the Hooghly. One large pinnace, with pantry, bathroom, sleeping apartments and parlour, and a smaller boat for cooking. Our crew consists of 16 men, 5 servants and our three selves. We are well victualled and armed and consider ourselves comfortable. The cruise is for health and I hope to God we shall obtain it. Money flies as you may well imagine—this unhappy affair has cost me £50 already.

I hope you see the papers regularly, for this insurrection is

74

The Lord's protection of the little band
at Arrah in the perilous times of 1857.

1 Emblazon'd in the Page of History
   Shall distant ages read & see
   How God can give the feeble victory
   Against their foes, how great they be.

2 Arrah's smale band can boast the hour,
   When their small spot God's shelter claim'd
   And midst fierce surges of Hell's pow'r
   Like Noah's ark unscath'd remain'd

3. On that smale spot who would not raise
   A Bethel to Jehovah's grace
   For where the Lord proclaims his pow'r,
   Should not His people meet to bless?

4 - Bless Him ye saints for all His love!
   Bow down ye rebels and obey,
   Our God the Son, as Sovereign Lord
   And yield subjection to His Sway.

23:d Oct: 1861   D.H.C.

This poem by Mr D. H. Chill of Alfred's staff refers to the so-called 'Siege of Arrah', mentioned by Alfred in his letter of 18 August 1857 and regarded by the people at home as an epic story of the Mutiny, told and re-told in verse and prose.

an unparalleled event and it is extremely interesting. From childhood we have listened with horror to the tale of the black hole in Calcutta when Englishmen were suffocated, but an occurrence like that would be but an incident among the atrocities of the mutineers. Surajah Dowlah, a century ago, was one villain whom we had to encounter—now we have a powerful host, Nana Sahib, Moor Singh and the King of Delhi.

When I last wrote I thought Mr Doyle and his party at Arrah had been murdered—circumstantial accounts of his being hanged in his own garden were published, but I am delighted to learn that he had fortified the house he lived in. The rebels besieged him and brought guns to bear upon the building but the Engineer and his trusty Sikhs aimed so well that the cowards dared not approach and battered the walls from a distance. During the four days he was beleaguered a detachment of 300 men of her Majesty's 10th Regt started to relieve them, but were surprised at night and were repulsed with a grievous loss—but another party with smaller force and a dozen Railway men, of whom Charlie Kelly and William Nelson were two, left Buxar for the same purpose, and attacking the rebels in flank, dispersed a large number.

Have you heard any of the unpleasant details from India? Among them poor Mrs M'how who fled from Shandi has some sad tales to relate. She was a doctor's wife and with her husband and child at a moment's notice had to leave her house; with no covering to her head she mounted a horse and a kind-hearted officer strapped her infant to his waist with his turban. The rebels were in sight and the few who started together soon were scattered. The officer who carried the infant lost command of his horse which galloped off and the mother did not see her child for three days.

Soon the husband and wife were left together and she saw that he could endure the heat and fatigue no longer. They stopped and she helped him from his horse—I think they had but one— and she left him to seek water in a little stream that was near. When she reached it she felt such pain from her legs having been burnt by the sun that she forgot her husband for a time and paddled in the water. Then she returned and having no cup she collected water in her wet garments and squeezed it over his face but it was useless and her husband died. She could not bury him but tied up his head with part of her dress and spread some leaves over him and left the place. The rebels overtook her soon and pulled her from her horse, searched and robbed her, tortured her until she besought them to kill her at once and then left her. How she reached a place of safety at last I know not but she managed to arrive at the Steam Wharf and shared a cabin with a lady friend of ours who had also to make a hasty retreat from a burning bungalow. The poor widow is nearly crazed. Many of these unfortunate people will die from the consequences of their hurried flight—I dare say as many as have been killed. To remain with so small protection was rash of Doyle, but the defence was gallant and the rescue heroic.

While we are surrounded with sorrow and yesterday's horror is only equalled by the account of to-day's atrocity, it does our hearts good to hear of all your quiet life—to imagine you the same as we left and to learn each particular of your peaceful home. I do so like to hear of your visits and visitations in Salmon Coloured silk and hope more Bermuda estates and more unclaimed dividends will keep the wolf from the door. I think you can scarce do better with part of the money than to pay off the mortgage.

Now do write nice letters for I dearly love to hear from you. Best love to Julia and Emily.

Ever your affect. Son,
Alfred.

Alfred has said that his salary was £500 p.a. Supposing that this equates to, say, £10,000 today we might multiply any figure he gives by 20. Thus £50 becomes more like £1,000 in our present-day terms.

Tantalisingly, there is no further reference to the financial windfall from the West Indies, for there now follows a nineteen-month gap in the correspondence.

A

FORM

OF

PRAYER AND THANKSGIVING

TO

ALMIGHTY GOD;

TO BE USED

In all Churches and Chapels throughout *England* and *Wales*, and the Town of *Berwick-upon-Tweed*, on *Sunday* the First Day of *May* 1859, being the Day appointed for a GENERAL THANKSGIVING to ALMIGHTY GOD :

For the Success granted to our Arms in suppressing the Rebellion and restoring Tranquillity in Her Majesty's *Indian* Dominions.

By Her Majesty's Special Command.

LONDON:

Printed by GEORGE EDWARD EYRE and WILLIAM SPOTTISWOODE, Printers to the Queen's most Excellent Majesty. 1859.

6

SAFFRABAD, MONGHYR - I

We left Alfred and his little family cruising on the Hooghly River, in considerable style, as they sought to regain their health. That was in August 1857, after which there must be a bundle of letters missing, the next one being dated March 1859, so that we are told nothing about 1858.

It seems that the family were back in Rajmahal (in the new bungalow?) by October 1857, because later on Alfred mentions buying a horse there in that month. Moreover, in the family Bible is the following interesting entry:

> Susan Emily, born 25 July 1858 in Begumpore,
> Nr Rajmahal,
> Christened 26 Sept 1858 in Bhangupore
> Sponsors: Robert Heenan, Susan Vaux, Emily Williams.

So we know, because Bhangupore is also near Rajmahal, that they were still there in Sept 1858. Of the sponsors, Robert Heenan is presumably a local friend or colleague and Emily Williams is of course Alfred's widowed sister. Susan Vaux has not appeared in the story so far, although henceforth she is occasionally mentioned. A first cousin of Alfred, but ten years older, she is the daughter of his uncle Bowyer Vaux of Birmingham. She, with her sisters Hannah and Lucy, compiled an illustrated account, written in verse, of a carriage tour through Gloucestershire the girls and their parents made about 1840. Almost certainly the elder Susan gave

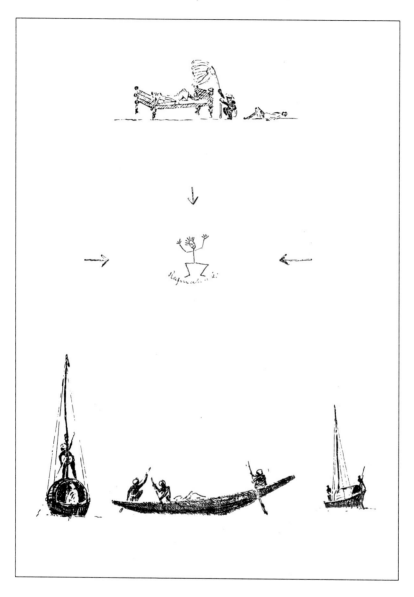

Farewell to Rajmahal.

this delightful souvenir to her god-daughter, which is how we come to possess it. At any rate, from now on Em and Alf had two children to write about.

Some time during the cold weather of 1858–9 Alfred was promoted and the family moved to Saffrabad, near a place called Monghyr, still on the banks of the Ganges. From books we have read, as well as these letters, it seems that everybody liked Monghyr and there was rather more social life than had been the case in Rajmahal.

Saffrabad Monghyr

13 March 1859, Monday

My dear Mother,

The weather still keeps cool and we are enjoying it. Em is as well as usual and the children in excellent health. Our garden is a delightful place for them in the morning and there is a nice grove of mango trees in which they can play until quite late in the day. Brickwood learns a little English and a little Hindustani and is happy watching the squirrels in the palm trees or playing with Cherry the dog. He has become no less unaccustomed to Elephants and is now rather frightened of them—it is his ambition to have a pony *Ghora* all to himself. Our roads are better than at Rajmahal where the rough stones made travelling disagreeable.

We were there so unsocial that now we can visit people we seem to have lost the inclination and are considered to be any stay at home quiet kind of people. In India folks mostly love display in the way of dinners, tiffins and any other assemblies when they may astonish one another with the appearance of those dresses on their persons which in their wardrobes have been so often exhibited and discussed.

You see a little plan of our compound, showing all the

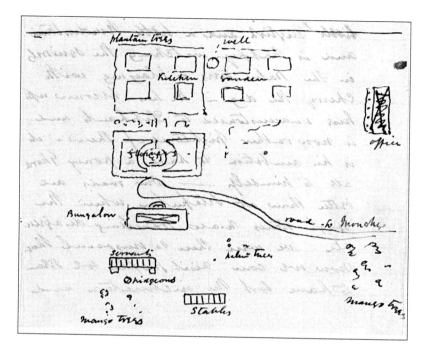

Sketch of Saffrabad Bungalow Grounds.

arrangements of office, bungalow and out-offices. The garden is of good size and in Indian fashion has a well in it. The gardeners draw up water in a pig-skin over a pulley, and at the edge of the well empty it into a trough formed of clay on the surface of the ground—and from this smaller troughs lead to each bed in the garden. As soon as one bed is watered its special trough is stopped up and another gets its share. Four men and a pair of bullocks do the job.

We were sorely tempted the other day to buy a piano. Mrs Tucker, wife of the Collector of Monghyr has just been confined and is going to Darjeeling for the hot weather and intends to go home next year, so all the goods and chattels are being sold off, and amongst the rest a Grand Piano, £80. Mrs Tucker is a musician and the instrument has been a fine one, but we decided that the money was too much, especially as pianos are spoiled so much by this climate.

Did I tell you that the increase to our pay of a quarter in addition to what has been promised for two years but withheld is now being paid and I expect to get some back pay? This is pleasant, for our life in India wants a little gilding besides what it has from the sun!

We have been reminded lately that the war is not yet over. Mr Evans, who was lately deputy chief Engineer under Mr Turnbull in Monghyr, and who was promoted a short time since to be the Chief Engineer of the Railway from Allahabad to Jubbulpore, was on his new charge in camp with three other engineers, his subordinates, surveying at the end of February. His camp was suddenly attacked by a large party of the enemy and the first intimation of the surprise was the rattle of musquetry and the bullets flying through the tent. They had a police guard who were cooking or did not choose to interfere, so all the gentlemen ran to their horses with the intention of escaping. Evans' horse unfortunately began to fight with some of the servants' Tattoos [sic] and he was thrown. Mr Linnell, a district Engineer lately arrived in the country was taken prisoner. Poor Evans was immediately speared through the chest but the other two, Campbell and Heywood escaped. Campbell after a time returned and found Evans' body without the head; he buried the unhappy man's remains and then rode to Allahabad to tell his widow—who is waiting there expecting to be confined with her fourth child. We in Monghyr have only her account yet and we have not full details of the sad affair.

Evans was always careful of himself and waited for official intimation that the country was safe and had only been out, after this had been given a few weeks, before he was cut up. We expect that some of Tantia Topee's cavalry [an accomplice of Nana Sahib] did the deed. And we now hear news that poor Linnell is dead. They have both left families to bewail Lord Clyde's foolish brag that the rebellion was at an end.

No more news except that my fever is gone for the time and that I send love to you all, but this last is not news.

Yr affect Son   Alfred H. Vaux

On the following Saturday Em wrote one of her rare letters to her sister-in-law, Emily Williams, but the two letters went by the same mail—'ex-*Calcutta* 22 Ma 1859'. Some details of friends at home have been omitted.

Saffrabad, Monghyr
18 March 1859

My dearest Emma,

I have left writing till the very last moment, hoping to say that I have received the expected little parcel. On the 14th we received a letter from Wilsons of Calcutta saying Mrs Halsey who was residing in his hotel had given him the order to dispatch the parcel, which was accordingly done on that day but as yet it has not come to hand. [Apparently only letters were automatically sent up-country but each parcel had to be authorised for dispatch.] Oh! my dear the post in this country is most worrying. The mail of the 4th of Feb was also in on the 14th but no letters have reached us at present. Perhaps tomorrow or Sunday we may have them. You may fancy how I have each morning watched for the *Dak Walla* and each time he only brought letters for Alf or the daily paper. Alf laughs at my impatience, so to punish him when it comes I won't let him have the first look.

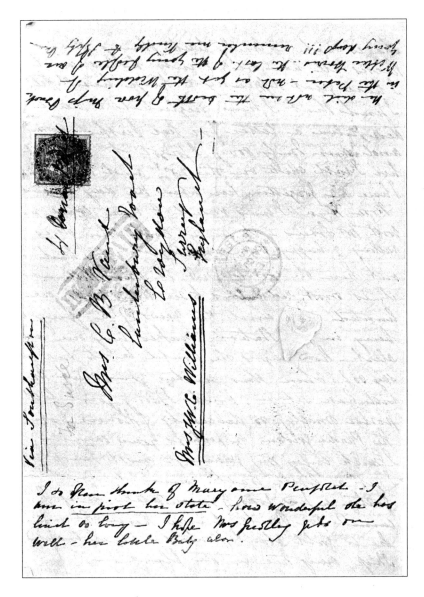

Em's letter to Emily Williams, c/o mother-in-law, which went by the Calcutta Mail on 22 March 1859.

There is no news of any kind to tell you. The weather becomes hotter every day and this last week we have had high hot winds—dust blowing in such clouds that we are obliged to shut all doors and windows, while everything feels gritty and the whole place wretched from the dirty appearance. To dust and clean is not of the slightest use—besides I am obliged to keep the children indoors as the dust is often most injurious to the eyes.

I think you may perhaps remember my telling you of a Mrs Orr, one of Alf's assistants' wife. Well, poor thing, 3 months ago her eyes became affected. She has been to Calcutta, had an operation and just now returned to her home, but is obliged to keep her eyes bandaged and sit in a dark room. She cannot distinguish her own baby from any other. It is said something had flown into her eyes and poisoned them.

To-day there is no wind and it is bright and clear. The natives have a great holiday, the 'Hole Pujah'. I do not know the origin of this festivity but the principal amusement seems throwing Red Powder over each other and getting very tipsy. Nearly all our Hindoo servants are away on leave to-day. We are not so much swindled by those necessary to work here as we were in Rajmahal but to-day my bearer had the impudence to tell me he required more oil for the lamps—having used 10 gallons in 6 weeks! and we use just three quarters of a pint nightly as we are never up after nine o'clock. No doubt he has heard that Alf has received an increase in salary and therefore steals accordingly! That is the way or *dusture* here.

Last Sunday Alf wrote a long letter to Mother and has I know told her about poor Mrs Evans. We are in great hopes that the Company may give her a pension, but it is not at all certain.

There is much illness about just now—Alf has had two days

fever again since he wrote but is better now. I am tolerable—indeed well for me though I had another attack on Wednesday morning quite suddenly. I had been chatting with Alf in the verandah before taking my bath and thinking how well I felt when all in a moment I was gasping for breath. I am stronger and far more happy in my mind feeling quite resigned to the Almighty's will. The children are fully well. Brickwood looks a little pale from the heat but is lively and full of mischief. Our baby girl also bright, rather worried with her top teeth just now. She is such a lively little thing, she kicks all her socks into holes and I have great difficulty to keep her supplied. I find that I have neglected to send dear Julia a letter for her birthday and am truly sorry I forgot it but tell her I will write on the 21st and she may know I have not forgotten her when the day arrives.

Poor Eliza, I was vexed to hear she was not with Mrs Lomax any more. It seems hard when she is willing and happy to be employed. If I had her out here she would not be Miss Eliza Wills for long! It is most ridiculous to see how girls are hunted up—the news of a 'young lady' being in a station makes everyone on the alert.

When this reaches you your sweet May will have set in and I fancy your little parlour smelling so deliciously of flowers from the garden. I much enjoy my garden, I get a little walk round it and gather some mignonette or if I cannot go Brick brings them to me. He is wild about flowers and would strip every tree in the place.

Alf has had a *Ton Phou* made for me, a kind of Bath Chair only carried by four men. I sometimes go out in this and I hope some day to go in the Buggy.

Before this reaches you Brick will be 3 years old. He enjoys his Mutton (without the chutney) very much now and should he return next year I can fancy I see him eating Sarah's bread and butter as long as she likes to cut it. Alf will not like to part with him, but I think whether I am permitted to bring him or not he ought to come home early—as he is so very delicate in his bowels. However, we do not talk of separation now as 'sufficient for the day is the evil thereof'. I am sure could Mother see Susan she would say she was 'Baby Julia' once more.

I hear heavy taxes are to be levied in this country on Beer and Wine and all articles of haberdashery and wearing apparel—so fancy what a price we shall have to pay.

Give mother my love and say we like the *Guardian* very much. I always enjoy the English papers.

Well dear, Good bye, with much love,

ever your affect sister Emily V.

A fortnight later they both wrote again, this time Em choosing to move the generations up one. Hers was a long letter, every item in the parcel being enumerated and exclaimed over, leading to detailed comment about people in England not known to us, so that much has been abridged.

Saffrabad, Monghyr
April 2nd

My dear Grandma, Aunts Emie & Julia,

This must be a letter to you all as I have the pleasure to say that the dear little Box has arrived. It reached here the very day my last letters were posted (19th March). I was dressing for breakfast and Alf was out on the line when My Boy came in with his heavy burden and said 'Three rupees to pay, Mama'. This was gladly paid and I felt as though there was to be no more dressing for me! However, I stifled my eagerness and continued my toiletry deferring the opening till my dearie came home. He has been so very busy but at last he came and when divested of his riding clothes, and lying down on the sofa to get cool, we opened it together, Brickwood standing by and indeed poking with his fingers. I assure you, when the books came to light he cried '*Dum awash*' (for sure) and forthwith sat down on the ground to examine them—then Papa and Mama were enabled to proceed in peace. In the first place we think the portraits capital and dear Mother is a beautiful likeness. I am afraid she is growing very vain—she looks so very nice!!! Dear Emie is looking better and stouter than when I left England—Alf, of course, thought her much altered— but we are delighted with them all. Next came the locket— please someone give Mother a hearty kiss from me!! The book markers are very pretty and I send many thanks to Cousin Maggie [not known] for them. The picture cards and books for Brick are most acceptable—although I fear the young gentleman shows but little wish to learn therefrom—he is not fond of his letters at present. The nice gauntlet gloves Alf declared he'd 'Bone'. I like them much and they are just what ladies wear here. The collars and ribbons are a nice shade and I feel almost lady like to have something really good. The little Box with hair-pins and needles sent by Kate is indeed most useful and I send love and thanks for it. The tape and elastic also most acceptable, particularly the pearl buttons as those we get here are of the commonest sort. Indeed dears there never was a wee Box so well crammed or the things so admirably chosen. The very Box I love to look at—as I remember it of old and fancy each and all of you three dear things. Many thanks and kisses for your kindness.

Alf is busy again and started yesterday at daybreak and will return I hope tomorrow. I cannot bear his absence for, putting aside my uncertain health, the country is not safe and it is the opinion of a clever man, many years here, that no European is safe 2 miles from his home. People have been far too sanguine both at home and out here. Poor Mr Evans and Mr Linnell's sad fate shows that. Just now rumours of all kinds are rife, how true they are remains to be seen, but people are very anxious again and many of the Railway Men are far from satisfied of their safety. So you see dear Mother I may well feel anxious.

The hot weather has now settled in and we are glad of *Punkahs*. I find it tells upon me much, though I am stronger. I still have those bad attacks often and Alf the other day said he thought he should send me home with Mrs Evans in July. I feel I must not have any wish in the matter—had I no children nothing in this life should separate us again, but with my two darlings it is my duty to see them home if possible. We shall see what happens, meanwhile make no comment unless Alf names the Subject.

Dr Dutton was here yesterday and ordered me Bitters and acid drops for a time. I hope it may prove of benefit, for I can take scarcely any food that digests. Dear Alf is better but has had bad fever last week, he is not strong the Dr says and it is excitement brings on the fever. The children are both well, Baby Sue such a little lively thing—she kicks holes in a pair of new woollen socks in one day. This is rather tiresome as well as expensive, as the cost is 2/– a pair for the wool only, besides my trouble in making.

Since I wrote I have been out three times in our Buggy with Alf. It shakes me a little but I hope to get used to it, as really I cannot breathe of an evening and driving there is always a little air. Now I think of you all with this sweet spring time and wonder if I should enjoy it as much now. I am constantly dreaming of being at home and not liking it—

doubtless I should miss the <u>large</u> dwelling house and grounds and the comparative freedom one has here, but I am going on the old theme again.

Brickwood eats well now. We dine at two o'clock. I wish you could see my Boy so solemn over his food, never disturbing himself let who may be at the table. In manners he is quite his father. A Mr Musson here says (he is a family man) that he never saw so contented a child.

<u>April 3rd</u>. We have just finished reading, the room is shut up, a *Punkah* in full swing and a wetted grass mat over one of the doors, so that in spite of a <u>very</u> hot day we are pretty cool and comfortable. Dear Brick and wee Sue are fast asleep. Dear Alf came back last night so I am once more at ease. Your next letter will I hope tell of Walter Harris's wedding—it seems odd to fancy a man so much older than we are <u>just starting life</u>, while we feel very old married people. Next Saturday it will be 4 years since Alf became a husband!

On the Table is a glass of flowers one of which is a lovely shaded lavender. I picked it myself this morning. Some of our flowers are very lovely and the colours are so vivid, but my <u>Pets</u> are a few sweet peas, a large scarlet geranium and some mignonette.

I do not know a <u>Mrs</u> Gouldsbury here, but <u>Mrs Ainslie</u> was a <u>Miss</u> Gouldsbury—I met both her and her sister when I was flying from the mutineers in 57. Perhaps Alf knows.

Have you seen . . .

Good bye, dears. Special thanks for the dear little Box.

Your very affectionate Emily V.

They must have been sitting there together that Sunday evening, writing their letters, for Alf begins in much the same vein as Em finishes hers. It is rather charming to notice that, as mentioned in other letters, it seems to have been their habit to read prayers together some time each Sunday. Neither mentions yet that Em is once more pregnant—perhaps they did not know themselves.

Saffrabad Monghyr
3rd April Sunday

My dear Mother,

We have read prayers and the children are asleep so we seat ourselves under the *punkah* to chat a little with you and the rest. A *kirkup tatty* is placed at one open door and all the remaining doors of the house are closed and the damp sweetly scented grass kept constantly wet makes the room cool and fresh.

Your and Julia's letters of the 3rd February arrived a fortnight ago and we are expecting another budget tomorrow or next day. The sympathy you both express for Em's suffering is very grateful, but of course to us out here you can do but little good. Dear Julia does not know what she thinks of undertaking when she talks of coming out here to be of service. I fear our pockets and her strength would not bear the journey and this country is a place in which generally the presence of an extra female, unknowing of the ways and means, is far from an assistance. We have our little ills to bear like other folk and must take the good with the bad without grumbling more than as English people we consider ourselves obliged.

Susan and Brickwood are in excellent health and spirits— the little girl as upright as an arrow with her blue eyes so wide opened that you see the blue as a circle with white all round. Your Indian grandson admires the portraits of Grannyma and Auntie Julie and is allowed occasionally as a great indulgence to take them from the table and kiss them.

Julia wrote to Em about a Mrs Gouldsbury here in Monghyr. I do not know who she might be, but a Mrs Ainslie, whom we met whilst in Bhangulpore is the daughter of old Gouldsbury the Commissioner of Rajshaya—he married a very dark lady who has borne him equally dark offspring. He is an old civilian drawing £3 or £4000/– a year but his good lady in former years was very extravagant and they now have to live on four or five hundred. Mrs Gouldsbury is the *Burra mem Sahib* and rules supreme at Darjeeling, the little station in the Himalayahs where on the borders of Nepal invalids from all Bengal endeavour to recruit. The good lady is both feared and disliked considerably but Mrs Ainslie and her little daughter are pleasant enough—Ainslie is a very clever civilian and a good racket player.

Uncle James and I have not exchanged letters for a long time. Will you please give my love to him when you go over to Sutton. My love to the girls, and believe me your affect Son

Alfred H. Vaux.

So the letters continued through the hot season, neither Alf nor Em apparently realising that an era in their lives would soon come to an end—although it was to emerge later on that Mother was not altogether surprised that this was so.

Saffrabad
18 April 1859

My dear Mother,

We do not seem to have much to write about this Mail. We have had some dust storms from the North-west and they have cooled the air quite pleasantly.

Em and I went out to dinner together for the first time since I do not know when [probably to the Club—they were not at all 'Club people'] and we enjoyed ourselves with Brickwood looking at some fireworks and a puppet show.

Your last letter was of the 19th Feb and told, from Kate, of the marriage of S. P. Pulham to Miss Bridges, both of them are known to one of the Engineers on my length here—a Mr George Smith—a gentleman who is always getting into rows and wanting others to extricate him. I am so sorry that Calvert has not arrived to cheer you up as you expected—but hope he still may be able to come over notwithstanding the large increase to his business which his new appointment entails [this must relate to Calvert's contract to design and lay out Central Park, NY].

I do not know about the house purchasing whether it would be better to buy it or not—if you bought it you would not like to move and you may become tired of that part of Croydon.

My dear little Boy is well and the upright clear blue-eyed Susan is noisy and happy, kicking and eating quite jollily.

My spouse will have told you of poor Mrs Vigors having to take her boy home and Mrs Orr at last being obliged to leave also on account of her eyes. Ours is truly a changeable life and I can quite picture Capt W. Harris' joy in escaping after such a lengthened sojourn as he has had in Burma and Hindoostan.

Emily likes to be driven out in the Buggy [a light 2-wheeled trap with a high seat for two. Easily turned over!] every evening and I am obliged! to indulge her and Brickwood to a family jaunt over rough roads. I have a young horse which I bought in Rajmahal eighteen months ago and have broken in to draw in harness and by the same token have broken three whips in the process, but he now goes pretty well slowly, steadily and with really a respectable jog-trot. So I have sent to Calcutta for a new set of harness and mean to be quite smart. We went out on a wolf hunt the other morning but were unsuccessful so must try again, for those brutes with the hyenas are so numerous that the villagers are alarmed—the children are so often carried away.

Now that your spring weather is so pleasant you will I suppose go over to Sutton again—mind you give my love to Uncle [James?] and Sarah—and to Julia too. Emily and Cuthbert are often in our thoughts and we hope one day we shall see the little people playing together. Good bye now dear Mother and remember me as your affectionate Son.

Alfred H. Vaux.

East India
River Ganges off Monghyr
Sunday 29 May

My dear Mother,

You have no letter from me last Mail so I must not be negligent now. It is a piping hot day, eleven o'clock, and Harris and I are sitting under the straw thatch of my boat while the men are cooking— wife and children at home three miles off and pretty well. Susan has a cough but only from teething I hope. She is a dear engaging little creature and to all appearances quite healthy thank God. Brickwood has his face covered with large boils and he teases his mother rather but I do not think he is ill—the great heat of the weather brings on the boils perhaps and he does not suffer so much as his disfigured swollen face would make one suppose. Em is not strong and very nervous when I am away from her more than two or three hours at a time. I do not like to leave her as it is quite painful to her to be alone, but I have had so much fever lately. The attacks have been so frequent and weakening that I am obliged to try some means to get stronger, so have hired a boat for a month to have occasionally the benefit of the river breeze; it always does

96

me good. People rather laugh at the idea of my leaving my comfortable home to be in a little boat, but that does not hurt me much. I took quinine regularly for a long time and I think it irritates the nervous system so much that I was rendered more sensitive by its use. Quinine is given in larger doses here than at home. I took 5 grains twice a day but sometimes 20 or 30 grains are given at once. Dr Daka is now administering arsenic and I think beneficially as I have had no fever since I began with it.

We had a typhoon last evening which nearly broke my boat to pieces on the shore, and as I rode to see how the family fared the roofs of huts and branches of trees strewed about gave evident signs of the force of the wind. But no harm had come to my dears.

These storms are grand but rather awful. The wind will be gently blowing from the east and all around will be bright when you see a darkness gathering in the north-west—not the blue-black clouds of an English thunderstorm but a thick darkness and you know what is coming, and make all tight that you can. The darkness rises still higher in the heavens and a yellow streak shows itself on the horizon, this increases until it rises as high as the sun appears ninety minutes after sunrise, but still the wind is from the east and all is clear. As the yellow dust draws nearer you see the feathery outline at the top whirling about and a dry breeze comes puffing now and then in your face. Then comes the *tufan* in full force—in half a minute the bright sunshine is obscured—the gloom increases instantly until you cannot see ten yards round you and the open moist pores of your skin are covered with yellow sand which the fierce wind blows quite through your clothes. Your skin is dried directly and your teeth as they move over one another sound like two pieces of sugar rubbed together, there is such a grit between them. Leaves and straw, branches and all sorts of queer things come whipping about you and in minutes the rain dashes against your side not in drops, as a mild well-disposed rain might be expected to do but in large masses of lukewarm water— if you are in a boat you do not observe much more because you have to jump out on the shore on which you have been driven and try and keep the side off the bank by pressing against it, and as the keel is first half out of the water in the fore part and then aft and big waves are tumbling over you this is difficult.

My pony yesterday was picketted under a tree on the shore and was nearly hurt—for a big bough fell just across his back and being fastened hind and fore legs he could not escape, but fortunately the chief weight of the wood came on the ground. The storm lasted two hours and gradually cleared off leaving a beautiful clear evening.

Emily will have told you about our gay wedding party and generally of anything which has occurred such as our friends and neighbours having whooping cough . . .

The rest of the letter is about mutual acquaintances at home, the possibility of another visit to Uncle James in Sutton and ends as usual

Believe me your ever affect Son
Alfred H. Vaux.

A month later poor Em was in trouble again, the result of what should have been a happy occasion.

Sunday 26 June 59
Saffrabad

My dear Mother,

Your and Julia's nice long letters of the 4 May came safely to us on Thursday—the little hymn book all right also and they were very welcome to Emily as your love always seems to give her fresh spirit. Poor girl she needs comfort just now for she is very weak—on Wednesday she miscarried and is now in bed doing pretty well but suffering much from face-ache or some nervous affection of the jaw—not one however I am glad to write which stops the action of her teeth—her appetite being excellent. Our little boy is sleeping by her side and is in capital health, thank God, rather troubled with boils which garnish his nose giving it a bulbous look far from ornamental, but still very well. Little Susan is teething and very thin in consequence but giving no trouble and enjoying her games and arrowroot heartily. Her 'die' is attentive to her and we are fortunate to obtain so quiet a woman. Wet nurses are proverbially a nuisance in India but we have had no disagreeableness with this woman and she has already been with us eleven months.

I have received since I wrote to you another instalment of my back pay which is acceptable but I think they might repay it altogether—I have yet to be paid £100 for 1857.

We have been obliged to be rather extravagant. Our dinner set I bought when Emily came out, and during our sundry and manifold changes the number and size of pieces became reduced sadly, at last a shelf annoyed I suppose at having to support so pitiful a burden, broke and down came the plates and dishes on the brick floor of the pantry. As poor Mrs Evans is selling off her goods, I wrote to her to ask if she had a dinner service to dispose of. Down from Allahabad came two boxes of nice china, white with gold and purple at the edges and I have £20 to pay—not actually dear for this country but a monstrous price too, though not to be begrudged the widow.

Of course we wanted to show our purchases so asked Mr & Mrs Harris, Mr McCann and Mr Mills to dinner on Monday and had a pleasant little party. We have very good servants here, so different from Rajmahal, so Emily had no fatigue in preparing the dinner but I think, although she rested all day, that it may have hastened the untoward event of Wednesday.

I hope Alfred Babington will succeed in Melbourne. We have had accounts of the English Stock Exchange and think of Mr Slater but I suppose he has no money ventured.

The rain is falling in sheets and I hope the settled weather is doing me good—I have had no bad attacks of fever during the last six weeks and trust I may have no more. I am very careful not to expose myself—if I have to go 100 yards I have a palanquin!

We have no news of interest to you as the rains keep us all pretty quiet. You have heard of the bad behaviour of our young European troops—actual mutiny though not called so.

Good bye my dear Mother – Yr affect Son
Alfred H. Vaux.

At the very end of the following month Emily felt well enough to write a long letter to her mother in law.

Many thanks for	Saffrabad,
that nice ribbon!	Monghyr
	July 31st 1859

My dear Grandmama,

This will reach you some time near your birthday [she would be 67] so imagine you hear the love and good wishes we shall express for many happy returns!

My dear husband leaves me to-day for his trip to Allahabad. He will be gone about 3 weeks and I trust the quiet and the river air will dispel all the fever that hangs round him. His baggage is at the *Ghat* and he now only waits the Steamer's arrival. I with the children am invited to stay with Mrs Harris at the Hill but I do not think I shall go. I suffer so much again from my heart that I must be quiet, for these last 4 days all the old sensations have returned and it is almost more than I can do to keep Alf in ignorance of it. There is <u>no cause</u> for it now. As I am hardly free from a most <u>severe</u> [word illegible, possibly to do with the miscarriage] doubtless I am greatly weakened in consequence. I think Alf is better than he has been for some time. Brickwood looks pale and dark under the eyes but somehow keeps always on the go and dear little Susan (one year old) is getting rid of those nasty boils—she is <u>very</u> thin. The other evening Mrs Taylor said in the innocence of her heart 'Oh, Mrs Vaux, Baby is just like you, <u>so</u> tall and thin.' Alf laughed at the compliment.

I have told Julia all our little news and besides which Alf wrote you a <u>long</u> letter. The only topic here at present is the coming wedding of one of our assistant Engrs, a Mr Blair Stewart. He is the son of a 'high degree' in Scotland and has 'dared' to fall in love with Miss Crump (no relation of 'Little Daisy') the daughter of an Indigo Planter, a rather pretty young girl of 17—with £10,000 to her name, <u>but</u> she has unfortunately a dash of the 'Tar Brush' as they say here, her mother being a half caste—quite black. Stewart's family are in high dudgeon and will not recognise the marriage at all—they say 'though the young lady may not be dark the chance is their children may be little niggers and what a stain to the name of Stewart of Stewart.' However, poor Blair has made up his mind and the wedding will take place at the Factory the other side of the river some time in September. The reason they do not come in to Monghyr to the church is that the Mother is so black they do not wish any remarks made—so have it quite private. It is very curious—one family here—the Father is a very fair Scotsman, the Mother a <u>little dark</u> but nothing to notice. They have 8 children 3 of which are as fair as possible and 5 nearly black, so 'it will out'. Mr Stewart is a tall shambling fair man with <u>very</u> <u>blue</u> eyes and a pink complexion and light curly hair—the lady is very short but a nice little figure, bright light olive complexion and fine oriental eyes. The wedding outfit has just arrived from 'Madame Gervais' in Regents Street and is reported to be 'most exquisite', as it ought to be for the cost of £300.

So much for my little chit chat—please give my love to Kate and kisses to her chicks, and with much love

believe me your affect Emily Vaux.

P.S. I am getting a stock of new underclothing made for the children in case I am being, or they have to be, sent home.

At the end of the post-script is a rather smudged sentence in darker ink, clearly added hurriedly afterwards. It reads 'Mrs E. Vaux [word illegible] for England next Mail'.

In fact, as the following two letters indicate, Em and the children *did* go off to England and must have sailed on a mail steamer leaving Calcutta about the end of August, shortly after Alfred returned from Allahabad. In the second letter there is even a hint that his trip may have been postponed after all. It all seems to have been arranged in rather a rush but perhaps—as has happened to us all 130 years later—Authority suddenly granted passages without any warning. Probably they would not have mentioned their plans to Mother until they knew they were firm.

Meanwhile, 'the dears' in Canterbury Road, Croydon, had been busy, even cleverly discovering a Mr Burn, supposedly coming out to join Alfred, who could bring a parcel—but of course by then Emily and the children were already at sea.

Saffrabad
1 October 1859

Dear Mother,

I have several home letters all in one envelope addressed to Em. I am so sorry that Julia and Emily suffer so much from toothache—your climate in Croydon is I suppose trying but you appear to keep pretty well and I dare say that elsewhere the others would suffer as much as they now do.

I have not seen the box and the cloak and the other little presents which Mr Burn has brought and it may be some weeks before they reach me as transport in India is so slow and uncertain. I rather want Mr Burn to come up to me here but I have two Engineers who are in excess of our requirements so, if they do not leave, he cannot come.

I have leave of absence for nine weeks and contemplate a trip on the river but it is difficult to get away. I am rather surprised that Mrs Hull should really establish herself in Croydon but she will prove another neighbour and although people may have peculiarities a feeling of relationship is pleasant to maintain. I have some disagreeable neighbours just now as the crops are rising round my house—seven hyenas have taken it into their heads to locate themselves in the corn and come howling round my garden about sunset in a most noisy and unpleasant manner—hyenas and partridges are both abundant.

My bungalow is lonely now and I have asked one of our young Engineers to come and live with me for a time and he will probably be here while I am away on the river.

I quite enjoyed Julia's long letter descriptive of James Edward and Charlotte's adventures. I like to know and share all the amusement and difficulties which may arise in your busy little circle—you always seem to have some little novelty to talk about. I have nothing here worth mentioning and the changes all

103

through India are so thorough and so frequent that we seem as if we were travelling through a country rather than residing in it.

This morning in consequence of invitations ten or twelve ladies and gentlemen on horseback collected at Mr McAllan's house at six o'clock expecting to have tea and toast but when we arrived we found nothing ready and so the people refreshed themselves with champagne—fancy that with nothing else, at sunrise.

I can't write to you about my own particular dear ones until I learn that they really have reached England. I can only recommend that they are very regular in hours and habits and not allowed to bustle about too much nor to visit except very rarely until the winter is over. I scarcely like to write at all either to or about them, for I keep thinking as my pen moves that they may be already buried at sea.

Good bye my dear Mother, I kissed your portrait on your birthday.

Your affect Son
Alfred H. Vaux.

River Ganges 16 October 59
My very dear Mother,

What a gad about you are! Just before I came on board the *Agra* your nice letter from Teignmouth arrived telling me the news up to the end of August. I am glad to see that you quite seem to have anticipated Emily's possible return, so you will not have been much surprised at hearing of her being on the seas and near England.

I am not at ease as I have not heard how she got on—five weeks tomorrow since her letter from Ceylon came. Burn writes to me that the homeward bound passengers went to the Oriental Hotel at Cairo while he was at Shepheards. So I might have heard from Suez or Cairo by that Mail and since then another mail has come via Calcutta and also one via Bombay.

I do not expect to be back in Monghyr again if this trip does me good for nine weeks. Mr Turnbull was very kind about my leave almost ordering me off and I think he was right, for since my last attack I have been very shaky. My constitution is not so elastic after long continued jungle fever as it used to be.

Your account of the Devonshire people was a nice one and I can quite believe that you enjoyed your 25/– worth—how cheap?

I have a young man living with me from that neighbour-hood, son of a clergyman six miles from Teignmouth, he is one of my assistant Engineers. I dare say Uncle Bowyer has heard of Mr Good. The son is nice fellow enough but not quite satisfied with the country.

I am always pleased to hear of my relatives and liked to know of Dr Keller and his visit.

What a queer description of Uncle E.C.B. and the fracas with 'Aunt Sally' you gave me—your much esteemed brother got what we Indians call '*Chooti*' sooner than he thought. But I suppose the Brighton air blew all the bad temper away very quickly—at any rate he would not get much sympathy from 'Sister Ann'.

Do write to me regularly and never mind about being in good spirits. I like it all grave or gay, dull or witty is all equally acceptable if it comes from his Mother to her

affectionate Son Alfred.

As Alfred sailed in the paddle steamer up—or perhaps down—the Ganges, Em, Brickwood and Susan were approaching Southampton. We do not know where Alfred spent Christmas 1859 and

New Year 1860, perhaps with friends in Calcutta, but the others were certainly with Mother, Emily and Cuthbert in Canterbury Road, Croydon. It would be interesting to know how Emily V. managed aboard ship with two tinies, aged three and a half and fourteen months respectively, remembering her miserable experience on the way out. The doctor had then said that she should have had someone to help her and one wonders whether she found someone on this occasion. Perhaps Mrs Evans travelled with her—anyway, there was no lack of widows homeward bound at that stage.

No letters have survived to cover the period when Em was in England—presumably she and Alf wrote only to each other—so that we cannot tell when they were reunited. We do know that George was born in May 1861, so that Em was presumably back in India by August 1860. Allowing for two and a half months travel each way, she cannot have remained in England longer than about six months.

So she returned to Bengal and 'dear Alf', leaving little Brickwood and Susan with their Granny and Aunt Emily. They were never to return to India, nor would they ever see their mother again.

It seems likely that Emily was back in time for the Grand Opening in October 1860 of the line to Rajmahal, as mentioned on the following page. This was only the second railway line opened in India. It will be noted that Mr Turnbull, whom we have met several times already (he was particularly kind during the Mutiny), was the Chief Engineer and Alfred Resident Engineer, Bengal. It should also be noticed that the work was commenced under a Governor General (i.e. of the East India Company) and completed under a Viceroy, India now having been brought under the control of London. That is why, in the last letter but one, Alfred referred to so many changes taking place.

Silver medal, now in the possession of J. H. Vaux, which was struck in 1860

Round the periphery: Prosper thou the work of our hands upon us
                          Prosper thou our hands work. Ps XC

Round the edge: Mr. A. H. Vaux, Resident Engineer Bengal
                     October 15th 1860.

The
East Indian Railway
Projected by
Rowland Macdonald Stephenson
George Turnbull being Chief Engineer
was commenced in the XVth year of the reign of
VICTORIA
James Andrew Marquis of Dalhousie K.T.
being Governor General of India
and was
opened to Rajmahal
In the XXIVth year of the same gracious reign
Charles John Earl Canning G.C.B.
being Viceroy and Governor General
AD
MDCCCLX

7

MONGHYR II AND CALCUTTA

It is a great shame that no letters have survived from the two years between August 1859 and July 1861. We know that Em was away for the first twelve months, travelling home with the two children, while Alf, after his nine weeks' local leave, returned to his lonely bungalow to await her return. He doubtless continued to be plagued by malaria, which he would have attributed to the unwholesome air of the riverside marshes—through which he was driving his railway line—for it would be many years before the significance of the anopheles mosquito was known, and nearly a century before the arrival of malaria suppressants.

We know too that George Crozier Vaux was born on 23 May 1861 in Monghyr, where he was christened the following September.

The next letter we have from Alfred is dated in July 1861 and, written on black-edged paper, refers to the death of an Uncle Edward who is not known to us. It is interesting that in those days, even in remote Monghyr, one kept a stock of suitable paper for use on such occasions.

Saffrabad, Monghyr

4 July 1861

My dear Mother,

Many happy returns to my dear Kate. When Julia and Emily wrote on the 18th May you were in Doughty Street and they were under the impression that you would write from London, so mentioned scarcely any thing about you or your movements, so that I know little of what you were doing in May—whether you were present at poor Uncle Edward's death.

You will long ere this I hope have received the note I wrote via Bombay on seeing the announcement in the paper. We were at the Harris's then and have since returned to our house on the plain.

Our boy is well thank God and Emily pretty well too but sadly annoyed by Prickly Heat.

On 1st July we saw the Comet [not Halley's] and not expecting such a visitor were surprised at his appearance after a thunderstorm. Our friend Galwey has left Jumulpore and I am very hard at work as a successor has not yet been sent.

Galwey takes home a small parcel and in it is a stone which I selected from a native dealer's store as being of a colour you often wear. It is intended for a brooch and if you will allow Julia to have it set in the best fashion your Croydon goldsmith can fix it I beg you will accept it and think of me on your birthday. The stone came from Banda in Central India and is I dare say very common, but the shade reminds me of my dear old Mother's cape and lilac ribands, so please like it. Another stone of a more costly description is sent also in case Emily may like it. I do not know whether she wears such things, but set in gold by the same man that makes up yours I think the green stone would look handsome in a shawl of a morning— but if the colour is not approved it need not be set and I will try to find some other appropriate little present.

My two darlings receive none the less thought since the advent of a third—give my boy a kiss and tell him he must love Susie and be kind to her or we shall be unhappy.

Our wet weather is not so oppressive this year as usual on
account of the high winds that prevail.

Now and ever yr affect Son,

Alfred H. Vaux.

Emily too was thinking of presents, for the following little undated
notes (written on each side of a very small piece of thin paper)
were found rolled up with the above letter. It is noticeable that
letters enclosed in parcels were always short and written very small
on tiny pieces of paper. One wonders whether some Customs or
Postal regulation restricted the amount of written material allowed
to be enclosed—as is the case today, in 'Small Packets' sent by air
to Australia.

Dearest Julia,

Emily will have a trifle to give you from me. I hope it may
be enough to secure a Book Subscription for a year or at all
events 6 months. Thanks for your dear letter. I hope to write
next time. Ever your affect Emmie V.

Dearest Mother,

Will you buy a frilly pretty cap or anything else and wear
it as a little gift from me. I am thankful to say I go on all well
at present and am much better in general health. My poor
darling still suffers from fever—and I am convinced he requires
sea air before any change will be apparent but the money—the
money!

Your very affect E. Vaux.

At last we have a letter from Alfred telling his Mother something
about George, who is now four months old. The letter has been
a little abbreviated because it is rather over fulsome about the new
baby!

Saffrabad

5 September 1861

My dear Mother,

The new grand steamer *Mooltan* having broken down in the Mediterranean and the *Malta* consequently delayed at Suez your 20 July letters have not yet reached us. We much wish them to give news of Calvert of whom we have not heard lately on account of the loss of the *Canada*.

You will have probably remained at Croydon satisfied for the season with your little excursion to Brighton and funds will hardly have allowed another change for Emily and Julia.

We are still delighted with our portraits of the dear children—our friends preferring the uncoloured one which is I think the best photograph. On every available occasion out comes the blotting paper case and casual visitors are doubtless bored.

Our George Crozier V. is growing well, giving no trouble whatever, except on rare occasions when he thinks himself neglected by the household. Even then he does not permit himself to be much inconvenienced by his efforts to draw attention. He lies on his back giving forth an occasional dry-eyed shriek and devotes the intervals to trying patiently to force both his fists into his mouth at once—and as the mouth is big enough for only one, this is a fruitful source of amusement. Now and then he will try to kick the *punkah* hanging three feet above him, and signally failing seeks to hide his discomfiture by uttering another shrill call. He is a good boy and was christened on Sunday.

Our weather is very trying and has knocked me up—in all August we had hardly any rain. A long course of intermittent fever has so disordered me that I doubt if the effects will ever disappear. I have asked for and obtained 3 weeks leave but to take Emily to Allahabad by river would cost £50 and nothing short of that would avail much—and I will not go without her.

Poor Heenan is laid up with Sciatica and I should think would have to go home. Mrs Harris and children will probably leave for England in early part of next year.

We are looking forward to the cold weather and trying to make our garden pretty. It is sad jungle now but ploughing and weeding are going on.

Good bye my dear Mother, give a kiss to my darlings, love to the girls and take a great deal of affection yourself from your ever loving Son Alfred.

P.S. after breakfast 5 Sept

Your letter of 19 July has come in to tell of your happy gathering of grand children and the fatigue you feel while playing with them. I hope the thin Kate will fatten under the influences of your good air, good food and your excellent example.

I sympathise with you in the loss of brightness of your best copper kettle during the little ones' picnic. It is said that the numerous fleas to be found in Turkey are a great blessing to the inhabitants as they force the people to scratch constantly and thereby promote circulation of the blood.

When I see my servants washing tea-cups in a finger glass, or cleaning a saddle with a table napkin, I thank my stars that I am blessed with a source of moral irritation doubtless as healthy to my mind as the Sultan's fleas are to his torpid skin. No more now.

Thanks for the elastic—so useful!

Yrs A. H. V.

Love to all, E. V.

Emily by this post has had a letter from Mrs White who expects her confinement.

Five months later, in February of the following year, with George now rising nine months old, Emily wrote a long letter to her sister-in-law, Catherine Withers. It will be remembered that she had married Robert Withers, lived at Winchester Hurst and had two or three children whom she called her 'chicks'.

It is clear that some communication from Croydon had infuriated Emily V., but from whom it came is not stated. It was unlikely to have come from Mother, who was too sensible and too well acquainted with Alfred's financial situation to have charged him with lack of generosity. Perhaps it was his widowed sister Emily Williams who, with young Cuthbert to bring up, may have been short of money. At any rate, so furious was the usually even-tempered Em that she wrote one of the best letters in the whole collection. As she herself would have put it—her blood <u>boiled</u>, the ink spots <u>flew</u> and the underlinings were so angrily scratched that <u>they made a hole in the paper</u>.

Camp,
Derarah,
Bengal
Feby 24th 1862

My dear Kate,

Your nice long letter reached me last Mail, I was very glad to have such improved accounts of the dear children's health and in fact of all belonging to you—the last letters from Croydon have been anything but cheerful and we are quite grieved at their not being able to make all things comfortable, as we can do but little to improve their income. Some kind (but exceedingly <u>absurd</u>) friends have given us the tolerably good income of £2000 per annum and I grant them that £2000 a year would be most acceptable would they as kindly

show us the way to obtain it!! Why that sum is more than our
Collector and Magistrate have! And I suppose did dear Alf's
health bear the climate long enough (which it will never do)
the utmost he would ever have would be a chief Engineer's
salary of perhaps £1200!! Things are quite different to what
the company led men to suppose and instead of gaining promotion men are having their salaries lessened—if they do not
like it they can leave!

I wish most heartily that we could come home. To live in this
unhealthy climate running great risks every hour of our lives, to
have to give a fifth of our income to support two of our children
which are separated from us, and to know that as our family
increases they must go to England—they cannot live here—is
not such a bright Luxurious life as our friends believe.

True we have all the common wants of an Indian life—but
very far from the comforts generally enjoyed by people in our
station or position. Our Table is exceedingly plain—we keep
no carriage and horses save what are allowed Alf for his own
travelling along the line. I cannot ride in a Buggy because I
am too frail, therefore most times I walk—or go in the Palanquin. Consequently I get no Evening Drives round the
Course as other ladies do—we have no handsome furniture, no
instruments;—in fact nothing but what is sufficient for a plain
household— and lastly but also not least, there is an addition
to our family every year which event never costs less than
£50—to say nothing of the family medical bills.

Do not think I am grumbling. I am perfectly contented with
what we have here, so long as I can manage to save a trifle in
case of ill health. We have enough to live on and keep quite
free from any debt—but for people to imagine us wealthy is
the greatest piece of nonsense ever heard or dreamed of and I
would wish those very sanguine folks to come and try a year

at the same cost and prices. I question if these friends would be much the better off for the change. I cannot help writing this to you because no doubt you with others have made this strange mistake and labour under the same delusion that your good brother and sister are 'big Wigs', no my dear Kate nothing of the sort, just quiet plodding folks walking up the same hill with Robert and yourself, only not quite the same chance of a nest Egg when we reach the top!.

And now having explained and set my mind easy, I will proceed to a more pleasant subject. I have been rather anxious about little Georgie (now nine months) this last week, his teeth cause him so much trouble and he has so much fever which is always serious in this country. Children certainly do manage wonders or they would never get through their little troubles in India. I hope he is better and that I shall soon see the little white pegs peeping through. You ask 'who is he like'—we think he is very much like Suzie—he is as fair as can well be—large blue eyes and (when well) rosy cheeks. Very pretty legs and well-shaped feet but his hands are just his father's. He is very bright, lively and intelligent and most people call him a nice handsome boy (and please Mama). He is a great comfort and blessing to us. I think Alf makes more of him than of either of the others and the little fellow quite understands the attention—at the very name of 'Papa' he shouts and kicks his little legs with delight.

I suppose you have heard 'the whisper' from Croydon—it is indeed true. For although I have behaved better this time than heretofore, and did so hope I might pass a year clear, Baby was nearly seven months this time and I never waited longer than 3 months before, so there is a slight improvement you see. Georgie's nurse, who thinks herself a very wise person says I shall not have any more after this next and really I think

4 is quite enough, don't you? [Alice was in fact born in August 1862, 6 months after this letter was written.]

Our new Padre Mr Lingley and his young wife have left us and gone to their house in Monghyr. We like them both, he seems a most earnest man, but we are afraid he is not suited to this country, like most others he is dreadfully disappointed at his prospects out here. His stipend is £350 a year with a house and horse allowance. Now this sounds very pleasant and comfortable, but he finds that is barely sufficient to keep an establishment, and so poor does he consider himself that a subscription has been made in the Station to buy him a horse and some kind of conveyance as he could not afford it himself. The climate has already had such an effect on his wife that she cannot walk twenty yards—when she should be out all day with the school and district visiting at home. Now she has 'expectations' and that always takes your thoughts away in this country. We have two very nice services every Sunday and we get on with the singing very well. Alf does not think Mr Lingley is active enough—his district is from Monghyr to Jamulpore where the great Station Works are. Here live numbers of men, women and children who cannot well come into Monghyr to church, so Alf hinted that a service may be given once a week in one of the empty rooms—the answer was 'When an Engine and Carriage is put on the line for me I will perform early service every Sunday morning.' This is a perfect farce, to think the Company would go to the expense of an Engine just to go five miles to say nothing of keeping the rest of the men in attendance. So we are not quite pleased, although we like the people individually.

I have just told Mother that my friend Mrs Harris and her two children left last week for Calcutta, which they leave in the good ship *Marlborough* on the 25th. A sad break up of home but her health was so completely worn that our Doctor said she would never live another hot season. She has been getting weaker and weaker every hour and worse still constant mis-carriages—3 in 5 months—so the Dr said another would surely kill her. Poor thing she was quite broken-hearted at leaving her husband and home—and he, poor fellow, it used to make me feel quite low to be in his company he was so cut up, at parting from his little children. She will arrive in June I suppose. Papa has sent his little Sue a work box which Mrs Harris has kindly taken charge of.

Have you seen the Photos that Alf sent Mother? If so you will be able to picture Monghyr.

Mrs West another of our friends has also left India. She sailed in the *Newcastle* and expects to be in London about May next. She has kindly taken a little parcel for me in which is a box of ivory letters for you dear ones—I could not get any-thing to send separately for each, so this must be a little present for Mama to keep and amuse all with.

Poor Mrs West is quite an elderly lady. She came to India just three years since to bring out her only son's bride and she was to always live with them. He died poor fellow about a year after his marriage leaving his wife and a Baby of a month old. He was in the same position as Alf but unfortunately not so prudent in money matters—so when he died everything was obliged to be sold off to pay debts and his wife and child left without anything. The mother had £50 a year, no more—people were very kind and opened their houses to them and the end was, before matters could be settled for them to return to England, the young widow married, a good match, a young Magistrate Widower with two young children the youngest baby not six months old! So after this the poor old Mother in law had to go home by herself. As her income is so very small she talked of taking a house at Southampton in company with a niece and keeping a 'Home' for Indian children. No doubt she will succeed for she is known to so many people, particularly among the Civil Service and she was so extremely liked by one and all—besides which she is so loved by little children and was such a great favourite among the little folk where she visited. Her little grandson and his two half brothers are to be sent to her till old enough for school and I believe Mrs Harris intends to give her two boys to her—when her health will allow of her joining her husband again.

I hope Mother and Julia may see her—she is first going to stay with her nephew Dr Corbould at Sydenham and promised to go over to Croydon and have a chat about us. She is a dear old lady and we are very fond of her and much regretted her departure—but that is always the way in India one meets good friends only to be parted again, and really an Elderly Motherly Woman is indeed a comfort in a Station. Mrs Harris too I hope some of you will see—she goes first to Hampstead and then to Poole in Dorset.

We are now in camp at a place called 'Dararah' about 10 miles from Saffrabad. It is very warm and we use an empty room in the new Station for the day and sleep in our tent. Alf has a great deal of work over here, and he cannot stand the long journey from our house, so we came here to save him all we can—not a splendid residence for a man of £2000 a year, just 4 brick walls with a table and 2 chairs!! But this is Luxury! Alf is off to Anu . . . [illegible] another 12 miles away and does not return till dinner, so I am having a famous gossip with you.

I have just remembered that you will receive this just about the eighth anniversary of your wedding day—accept good wishes for health, happiness and prosperity. We are getting old

<u>Matrons</u>. Alf received the little [illegible] Robert sent him. We are glad to learn godson Johnny thrives. Give all the chicks a kiss from their Auntie in India. I am so glad dear little 'Button' improves but I expect you are a <u>wee</u> bit tired of this long scribble so will conclude with kind love to husband and self.

Your affect sister Emily E. Vaux.

This is Emily's note that went with the previously mentioned little work-box from Alfred that Mrs Harris took home for Susan, who was now nearly four years old.

My dear little Sue,

Have you seen your nice Work box that Papa sent you? Mama hopes you will like it and soon be able to make a Pocket handkerchief for Auntie Emily. Brother George is very well and sends love and many kisses to his dear sister. He can hop about nicely now holding Papa's finger and can say Mama and Papa. He is such a happy little boy you would be so fond of him. Mama hopes some day to bring him to England—then how happy you will be to see Papa, Mama and little Brother. God bless Mama's Suzie says dear Mama in India.

And a few weeks later comes the letter that everyone in England must have been waiting for.

Monday 25 August 1862
Saffrabad

My dear Mother,

We venture a line by the Bombay Mail [i.e. faster and more expensive than the usual Calcutta Mail] to tell you that a daughter was born yesterday morning at half past eleven. Emily and the child are both doing well thank God. We had just

time to send for the doctor and complete all preparations
before the birth.

There is nothing much to tell you about the little one's
features [i.e. Alice] more than that the voice is certainly to be
heard occasionally. When she is about again Emily will write
particulars.

Saturday was a gala day for the people of Monghyr as Lord
Elgin paid a flying visit in the afternoon. I did not appear but
his Excellency nevertheless expressed himself highly gratified
at every thing and every body. We expected a lady to arrive
on Saturday evening to stop the night and go on to Patna by
special train on Sunday [i.e. the day of the birth], but fortunately she could not come to our house but remained at the
Magistrates. We should have been inconvenienced by having
a *burra mem*, two children and an infant beside ourselves at such
an inopportune moment.

Good bye, with best love
Yr affect Son Alfred H. Vaux.

The above letter of 25 August 1862 is the last we have from
Saffrabad, Monghyr, and it appears that shortly afterwards Alfred
was promoted and moved down to Head Office in Calcutta, taking
his family with him.

We would not know the date of this move but for one of
Alfred's staff, Mr D. H. Chill. He was a poet who, in 1861, wrote
a piece entitled 'The Lord's protection of the little band at Arrah
in the perilous times of 1857'. This referred to the attack on the
Engineers and 'their trusty Sikhs' mentioned by Alfred on page
76. Mr Chill now wrote to Alfred and Emily enclosing a valedictory poem of farewell. His letter was dated 24 November 1862.

Suffrabad 24th Nov. 1862

To
Mr. & Mrs. A. H. Vaux –

Our dear Christian friends!

Seeing, that your departure from our midst will soon take place, – we cannot allow you to go, without a Token, that will at all times assure you of our kindest regards and our sincere respect and sympathy for you.

To be assured, that your memories are engraven on our hearts, for all the kindness which you have done to us, and that we esteem you dearly for your love to Him, whom the World despises, but whom we love, – will, We are certain, be to your intelligent minds, more acceptable than any thing else, – and more than all the platitudes of pompous Eulogies that can be used by inferiors in their valedictory address to their superiors.

We therefore beg your kind acceptance of the Enclosed few Stanzas, which have been Composed in Earnest simplicity, Expressly for the occasion.

With best wishes & kind regards, Believe us to remain, Ever yours Sincerely.
(David Henry Chill.
and Matilda Chill

For Mr & Mrs A.H. Vaux with the kind regards of Mr & Mrs D H Chill

Stanza 1.
Farewell dear friends! since duty bids you go,
Perhaps to scenes where kindlier feelings flow:
Farewell! and may Jehovah's arm protect
And bear you ever as the Lord's Elect.
You've known His name;— you have His goodness try'd;—
You've made His worship your delight and pride:
And if to own Him, none can be deny'd;
His care, your constant welfare, will provide.

2
'Twas near that Throne, where Mercy bends His Ear
To hearken mildly to th' suppliants prayer;
That tokens, surer than Masonic signs,
Past in sweet sympathy, in telling lines:—
They told of friendship deeper far than aught
Of surfaced friendship by the worldling sought;
They told of friendship that can never cease,
But grows sublimer on to Endless peace.

3.
Time and events may scowl and strive to part
The friendship thus begun, and freeze the heart;—
But though ungenial blasts may make it scant,—
It must revive to be a healthy plant;—
Sown, at the Altar of prayers sacrifice,
And by, one Faith, one hope, to reach the skies:
Not heeding the mere trifling incidents
Or poor Ephemerals of past events.

4
What can we wish you more, our Christian friends?
Than those sweet blessings, which from Christ descends;
For you to feel that when your cup o'erflows,—
To Him you owe it, who alone bestows:
To trust alike His pow'r to help in Time,
And lead your souls to reach the Goal sublime:
To find when Time has ceas'd, that you are blest
With all your dear ones, round Christ's Throne, at rest!

Again Farewell! and may the God of Grace
Both now & Ever deign your path to bless.
D.H.C.

Suffrabad
16th November 1862

122

It is more than six months before we see the first letter from
Calcutta, from Alfred to Susan for her fifth birthday.

Calcutta

5 June 1863

My little Sue,

Your dear Mama and I were very pleased with your letter and
I write to tell you on your birthday that we love you very much
because Aunt Julia sends pretty messages from you and writes that
you are a good girl. May God bless and preserve you. You and
Brickwood have had measles but we hope are both well again.

Little George and Alice also send their love to you and
would be delighted if you could take care of them in their walks
during the cool evenings. During the day the weather is too hot
to allow of little girls and boys being in the open air.

When you see Mrs Purdie be sure to thank her from me
for her kindness to you and Brickwood, and ask Cuthbert also
to write to tell Uncle how he likes school
and being with big boys.
We have such funny birds in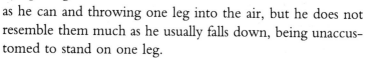
Calcutta called Adjutants which
are as tall as men and have
huge beaks and long legs and
perch on the tops of houses.
George tries to imitate them
by opening his mouth as wide
as he can and throwing one leg into the air, but he does not
resemble them much as he usually falls down, being unaccustomed to stand on one leg.

Good bye my little Sue—your affectionate
father—Alfred H. Vaux.

Hardly any other letters survive from the time the family was in Calcutta. We have seen that Alice was born on 24 August 1862, a few months before they moved down there, but we do not know where they lived. The *List of Europeans in Service of East India Railway Company* shows 'Jan 1863 Vaux Resident Dist Engr Monghyr. On R 800 + £5 premium' and 'June 1863 Vaux Asst Chief Engr, Chief Engr's Office, Calcutta. On R 1000 + £5. Life Policy £11.17.0'.

The family Bible kept by Em tells us that Harold was born a year after Alice, on 11 August 1863. He was baptised by his father and died on 26 August.

Poor Emily never achieved the 'one year clear' which she mentioned previously she so yearned for, for on 3 August 1864 Power John Vigors Vaux was born in Calcutta; he was to be known as John. The christening was on 11 September and clearly the great Mr Vigors was present as godfather. Vigors had been Alfred's first boss at Rajmahal (and on return from furlough had reclaimed his official quarter, to Emily's disgust) but was still there as 'Dist Engr', so Alfred had caught him up when at Monghyr and had now overtaken him professionally. Much later on, as will be seen, Vigors is found staying in the Vauxes' house in Simla as he tries fruitlessly to obtain another appointment.

A few months before this last birth Em wrote a slightly confused letter to her sister-in-law Emily, of which only the first page remains. 'Our dear boy' would be her eldest son Brickwood, whose birthday was on 23 April, but Maggie is not known to us— perhaps one of Kate's 'chicks'. Alfred must have been working very hard if his three days' holiday was such a treat for his wife.

21st April 64

Many many happy returns of this day to you darling. I

thought of Kate yesterday and shall not forget our dear boy and Maggie—23rd and 24th.

Dear Alf has been at home for holiday (3 days) such a treat for me. He read the 'Small Horse' to me yesterday while I was busy mending!

There is one more letter from Calcutta, from Emily to her children Brickwood (eight) and Susan (six). It is undated but appears to have been written soon after John's birth in August 1864, and is the last we have in Em's handwriting. The PS confirms our theory that the children are living with their aunt, Emily Williams, and her son Cuthbert, who is the same age as Brickwood.

My dearest Brickwood and Suzie,

I can only write a few lines this mail, just to tell you your new little brother is quite well. He is a fat little fellow with dark blue eyes and hair like Auntie Katie's.

Dear brother George is not very well and has to take much nasty medicine—but he is so brave—he holds the wine glass for me and then drinks the bitter stuff without a word! Sister Alice has had bad boils over her but is again better. She is very happy here playing with some little puppy dogs—and today Mrs Pussy has given some jolly little kittens—Alice is delighted.

Papa sends love and with much from me

always my darlings

Your own Mama   E. Vaux

A wee kiss from Baby.

Please give Auntie Emily's love to Cuffy.

It is disappointing that the health of the children seemed to be no better down in the Ganges delta than it had been up-country. As for the parents, Em's heart condition was as unlikely to have improved as Alf's malaria, now chronically intermittent wherever he lived.

Alfred was approaching ten years unbroken service overseas and was due for home leave. This was planned for the following year, and passages were booked for late May 1865.

Mooltan, P & O liner built in 1861.

8

HOME LEAVE

It is not hard to envisage the excitement in both Calcutta and Croydon as the time drew near for the family to sail for England. For Alfred there would at last be a break after ten years in India and for Emily the pleasure of travelling with her husband, having three times made the journey alone. Ahead of both lay the joy of seeing Brickwood and Susan again after six years' separation, only tinged by the distant prospect that George, Alice and John would have to be left behind too, when their parents returned to India. As for those in Canterbury Road, the eager anticipation and frantic preparations can well be imagined. There might too be a natural apprehension on all sides that the writers of those many letters might turn out to be rather different in the flesh than in imagination. Em had once told those at home that she sometimes had bad dreams of returning to England and *not* liking it.

The date selected for departure, late May 1865, was not particularly auspicious and was perhaps chosen to suit the Company rather than the family. Its only merit was that it would bring them to England in the warmth of mid-July. On the other hand, it would keep them in Bengal until well into that trying part of the hot season before the coming of the rains. Worst of all, it would bring them into the notorious Red Sea at midsummer when, it was said, seamen had sometimes been driven insane by the scorching wind and blazing sun.

Alfred did not keep a journal, but he had a pocket diary in

which he would pencil occasional notes. He did so now, on a couple of pages which he later tore out and kept. They read:

<u>1865</u> June

15 Thursday	Very rough weather
16 Friday	Very rough could not go on deck
17 Saturday	Very rough could not go on deck
18 Sunday	Calm weather, but very hot, dry and bright
19 Monday	Aden
20 Tuesday	Left Aden
21 Wednesday	My poor wife died at 9.20, buried at Sunset off Zebayer

There are no further entries but, taking pen and ink, Alfred wrote out in a firm hand, and pinned to the loose sheets of the diary, the following statement:

There is no statement of what caused Emily's death, but the indications are there. There does not seem to have been a long or serious illness, or she would have been put ashore in the hospital at Aden. We know that she was a very poor sailor who became dreadfully ill 'whenever the ship moved', and for several days the *Candia* had been tossed by storms so rough that nobody could go on deck. Battened down below, the atmosphere in that heat must have been almost unbearable. One can imagine Emily feeling better on Sunday, as the weather calmed and next day the ship anchored off Aden harbour. But one more stifling, plunging night was too much for that brave but already strained heart.

So Alfred and the little ones (aged four, three and eleven months) had to finish the voyage by themselves. One wonders how he managed as they crossed Egypt, put up at the Oriental Hotel and at Port Said boarded the *Syria* for Southampton. The children would have been a handful for two, let alone a mere man on his own. But somehow they got there.

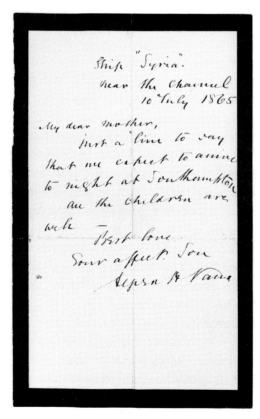

Soon after he and the children arrived at Croydon Alfred received a letter from a Marion Crozier, who must have been godmother to little George. This gives us the first indication that there had been any mishap to the *Candia*.

> Claremont Hotel
> Penge Lane
> Monday July 31st/65

Dear Mr Vaux,

The contents of your letter greatly shocked me and more so as I had so lately received a letter from her before you left Calcutta.

It must be a great happiness to you that you were with her at the last and that she died peacefully and gently. We had read the account of the vessel stranding in the paper and then we feared the shock might be too much for her. It must be a great consolation to you that you have your dear mother and sisters to take care of your children. I can imagine the blank you must feel with the loss of such a wife, indeed I feel as if I had lost a sister having been at school with her and my parents having known her from a child. My dear father always loved her so on account of her kindliness and sweetness of disposition. I hope the Almighty will give you strength to bear up with your loss. The troubles we have had in our family seem to have quite prostrated us. That my dear father is no more seems like a dream to me.

I have just returned home or should have answered your kind letter before. Mamma, Nellie and myself will call and see you next Sunday evening, as you mention you are engaged in the daytime, if agreeable. I am very anxious to see the dear children.

Mamma and Nellie join me in kindest regards to your Mother, sisters and yourself and love to the children.

Believe me

Yours very sincerely

Marion Crozier.

Before the suggested visit could occur, however, there was one more blow in store for Alfred. On Friday 4 August, baby John died—this was the day following his first birthday and less than a month after arriving in England. There is nothing said about the circumstances of his death, other than that it occurred in Croydon.

We do not know how Alfred occupied himself during the six months' leave, but it seems pretty likely that he would have spent most of it with his mother and the children. For the last few days he went on a little holiday with his sister Julia, and then on 4 February 1866 he sailed once more for Calcutta—alone.

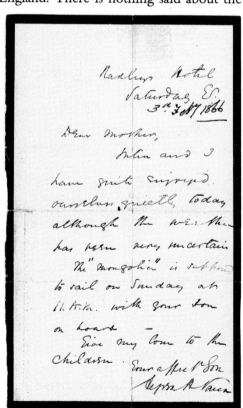

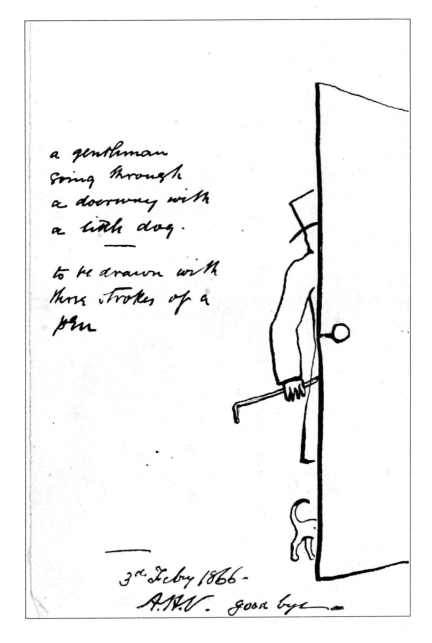

a gentleman
going through
a doorway with
a little dog.

to be drawn with
three strokes of a
pen

3rd Feby 1866 -
A.N.V. good bye

PART II

9

CALCUTTA AND SIMLA

Correspondence covering the second phase of Alfred's married life is less comprehensive than that for the first—and much less easy to follow. Perhaps Alfred did not write so often to his mother, as now he had the children to write to as well. The second wife, Caroline, apparently did not know Alfred's family as well as had Emily Vaux and so the few letters we have from her to Canterbury Road are in a different style. It would not have been surprising if Mother and the sisters, who had been very fond of Emily Vaux and now had her children to care for, had not resented Alfred marrying again. Then, of course, a new family was being produced in India and one can see Alfred consciously trying to bridge the gap between those at home and those out there. There was more movement, too, Alfred being in Calcutta for long periods while his wife and children were in Simla. There is also evidence that at some time Emily Williams moved to East Anglia, taking Brickwood with her, and that Suzie joined her godmother Susan Vaux in Teignmouth. That would have left George and Alice in Croydon with their grandmother.

Letters from the first three years being so few, the sequence of events during this period is shown below:

4 February 1866   Alfred sails for India, presumably arriving in May, thus completing one year's leave of absence.

3 January 1867   Alfred in Calcutta, with no indication that he is returning to UK.

29 October 1867   Marriage to Caroline Hollins, in UK.

5 July 1868   Alfred and Caroline at sea *en route* to India.

25 August 1868   Frederick born in Calcutta—he must have just missed being born at sea.

8 March 1869   Frederick dies in Calcutta.

There are only two short letters from the period of Alfred's widowerhood in Calcutta. The first of these is written on rather nice black-edged paper, embossed with the family crest—he must have brought it from home. He may have paid a nostalgic visit to Monghyr, for now he sent Alice a photograph of their old bungalow there. What a pity that Brickwood's scrap book is missing. It is interesting that Alice or someone else (she was just four) wrote on the letter 'Rec'd 11 Decr 1866'. So that particular mail took fifty-one days to reach England.

28 October 66

Calcutta

Dear little Alice

How is dolly Rose? Not fallen to pieces yet? Please to present my best respects to her and thank her for amusing my little girl.

Brickwood will paste a photograph of the old bungalow at Saffrabad in the book for you: tell him that the paste should be made thin with arrow root. You must take great care of the picture because you will like to see it when you grow to be a great girl.

God bless you my darling

Your affect father   Alfred H. Vaux.

In the New Year of 1867 Alfred wrote to his sister Emily Williams.

Calcutta
3 Jany 67

My dear Emily,

I received your letter of the 23 Nov on New Years Day [so that took only 39 days] and first admired the pretty quaint heading and afterwards was gladdened by the kind spirit in which it was written.

I also received a note from Doctor Collins who had seen my children, but my latest from Julia is the 16 Nov received some weeks ago [weeks? he must be very ill].

Your good wishes for my health were poorly fulfilled for I have had and have as bad an attack of fever as I ever suffered from—the port guns, fired at midnight dividing the two years, were heard by me as I lay in bed racked with pain in every bone and nerve—I have not gone downstairs for 5 days and am very ill. On the 1 Jan I had arranged to go to visit a friend about 400 miles from this who is living in a pleasant hilly country, but of course I could not go.

Ten days ago I sent a servant to 'lay my dawk' that is to arrange for the journey, have palanquin bearers on the road and so forth. He is waiting now and wondering.

My last to you told of my position and neighbours. The two ladies and their sons are very well thank you.

I read a great deal of travels and other light reading and completely forget almost all. Lord Dunkellin's book I remember well when it came out. His Latin speech is rather too good to be impromptu.

Good bye, give my love to Cuthbert.
Your affect brother,
Alfred H. Vaux.

Mrs Caroline Vaux (née Hollins) ('Carrie') (1840–1910),
Alfred's second wife (taken in Simla in 1869).

It is surprising to find that Alfred spent only about a year in India before he was back in England for another leave.

From various sources we know that he married Caroline Hollins on 29 October 1867 but we have no other particulars. Nothing is mentioned of her family nor when and where Alfred met her. We know only that Alfred returned from India for the wedding at Christ Church, Croydon. He would hardly have had time to get back to England after the above letter was written in January 1867, find a wife and marry her before the end of October, so one must assume that he had met her during his leave the previous year and now returned especially to scoop her up. I have been unable to discover her age at this time, but have the impression that she was quite young. The idea that Alfred met her in India, married there and brought her home to meet the family is attractive but does not wash—it is clear from letters which follow that she had never before made the passage to India in either direction.

In February 1868, after his marriage and whilst still in England, Alfred wrote a little poem to amuse the children.

> As George and Alice stroll around
> the fields near Duppas Hill
> They search the hedge rows ditch and ground
> and streams at Haddon Mill
>
> They move with eager hand and eye
> and stealthily they tread
> in hopes to see a butterfly
> with painted wings outspread
>
> See George is here with Susie's net
> and little Alice watches
> She likes the fun but pities yet
> the butterfly he catches

As George and their stroll around
the fields near Duppar hill
they search the hedge rows ditch & grow
and streams at Waddon Mill

For George will sometimes tear the wings
which sparkle like a jewel
while Alice cries 'Poor little things'
'How can you be so cruel.'

February 1868

By the end of June 1868 Alfred had had at least eight months' UK leave and he and his bride were off to India. From Malta he wrote to Alice (nearly six), mentioning Brickwood (twelve), Susan (ten) and George (five).

SS Peru   5 July
off Malta

My dear Alice,

I must write a note to my youngest dear little girl as I wrote to the eldest boy from Gibraltar.

I send my dear love to you as does Mama who is very sea sick and uncomfortable.

The weather is fine and hot and the sea so blue, much more blue than your frock with the white spots. Tell Granny that we have had a fine voyage and tell Cuthbert we still have the geraniums in full bloom on the table. Dear Susie will be having her holidays from now—give my love to her and Georgie and tell them I will write to them, and tell Auntie Julia that I have been very well ever since I started. I have met several old shipmates on board among the officers.

Good bye my darling, God bless you—
Your loving father Alfred H. Vaux.

Having left the SS Peru in Alexandria, Alfred and Caroline (whom he called 'Carrie') crossed Egypt and embarked in the SS Mooltan at

Suez. Three weeks after posting the above from Malta, Alfred wrote a very long letter to his sister Emily. Only part is reproduced here.

SS *Mooltan*
Sunday. 26 July 1868

My dear Emily,

We have just had service on the quarter deck and I can do no better than chat with you. The day is fine and Carrie is lying on a bench on which is also my paper and I am sitting in my cane chair. The ship is rolling steadily: it is the same ship as that in which last year I sailed from Alexandria to Southampton so I know most of the officers. We have a warmish but on the whole favourable passage down the Red Sea—an uncomfortable day at Aden while the ship coaled, for there being no rain in that part the coal dust is very fine and penetrating. On Monday last we had the first taste of the south west monsoon and we certainly for three days and nights were pitched and rolled about in a most uncomfortable manner. The ports were closed and we, indeed nearly all the passengers, were sea sick. Soon the sea rose higher and I was sent spinning out of my berth with the back of my head on the edge of the wash basin. Carrie was more fortunate as she was, at every roll, brought up against the side of the cabin. I did not attempt to sleep again in my berth but lashed the square black box to Carrie's berth in such a position as to have about eighteen inches space between one corner and the corner of a fixed what not. Into this space at night I wedged myself with pillows and thus escaped much banging about. The side of the ship leaked a little under the severe blows of the sea and small rills traversed the deck which gathered and were disagreeable towards morning. Of course sleep was out of the question for either of us.

We thought that the ports being closed was unpleasant but worse came when the big seas struck the side of the ship, rose over the deck and poured in floods through the skylight into the saloon. The side lights above the deck were closed and then the flaps, but when the windsails [he means the canvas air scoops] were withdrawn and all above battened down the passengers were in the saloon with no air except what came from one small end door and we really felt miserable, bruised, without sleep or rest, with no power to eat or courage to face the storm of the upper deck. I never knew the monsoon to have raised so troubled a sea for so long a time. Before we all collapsed, but when we were thinking of a continuance of the same very heavy weather across the Indian Ocean the sea and wind moderated and we are all now pretty well again.

The ship is longer than the *Peru* and is not nearly so sea worthy: it is narrower and rolls and tumbles about in a most trying manner. I do not think that we were in much actual danger except one morning when a green sea dashed down into the stoke hole, breaking the gauge glasses and causing an escape of steam. If for any cause our machinery had become disabled then our position would have been most critical. Mr Power started from Calcutta in this ship last month and she did break down for two days in the Red Sea. Happily our engines now appear to be all right.

Mother has I dare say told you of our arrival in Egypt when I took Carrie to see the sights of Cairo—she suffered from the heat but was very pleased at the strange places.

Our passengers are not numerous but we have some little comedies different from those seen in English county towns. We have a young Read bound for Calcutta, a noisy good-tempered sharp lad, nephew of the tall ladies we used to see at Tulse Hill. On the strength of his great aunt having married

my uncle we consider ourselves relatives. We have also a Mr
and Mrs Byrde, Ceylon people, the latter a Hythe lady who
knows the Freeths intimately. This lady is taking out her niece,
pretty, sedate and eighteen. She also has the care of a young
Irish lady, bright, black-eyed, sharp, very religious and 22,
Charlotte Furnier, engaged to be married to a widower much
older than herself whom she has not seen for several years and
only in the first wife's lifetime. A few hours before embarka-
tion another young lady, Carlotta Harper, was added to her
string unexpectedly—a tall lackadaisical, slim, weak eyed girl
of 26, high-nosed, wilful, with a good complexion and floating
hair looking much younger. She is lately from Yarmouth, has
sat under Bowyer Vaux and knows his family [this is Revd.
B. Vaux, vicar of St Peter's, Yarmouth]. These three are our
spins, but we have our bachelors!

Now follows a description of these (British, Cuban and Portuguese) and the jealousies aroused by the presence of the various
ladies.

The long-limbed Carlotta, who anticipates with fear min-
gled with repugnance a meeting with a Ceylon civil servant
to whom her friends have allotted her, has long since sought
distraction in the sedulous attention of a good looking young
Portuguese gentleman whom we took on board at Gibraltar.
He travels to the East as a consul. Long, indeed unending
conversations relieve the monotony. In bad weather in day
time the floating tresses trail while the fair head rests on his
knees, the high nose appears above the table as she reclines on
the bench, the weak eyes are closed and the fresh complexion
(for the rouge pot is upset) is pallid. At night the attentive
swain sits at the door of her cabin with his life belt girded
round him to calm her nerves to sleep. In fair weather how

interesting it is to watch the flashing eye and curled moustache while his lips recount many adventures, for our Portuguese is a traveller. It is said that the Signor has twice proposed but she says 'No, I have given my word to one gentleman, true if circumstances were different etc etc.'

Another spinster has her little romance likewise. Bound to marry a gentleman much older than herself, of whom she knows next to nothing, she day by day has permitted her distaste to grow upon her. In the Mediterranean this was shown principally by her constant perusal of good books, but the place, the hour and the man arrived—Suez, tea time and Lieut Shelley Leigh Hunt, who for eight months has served his country well in the useful but prosaic post of Commissariat Officer at Suez to the Abyssinian expedition, to whom he has been shipping stores, mules and donkeys.

Ground was broken by his showing Carrie and me a very curious bible in Abyssinian characters written on parchment and enclosed in a leather case smelling loudly of mutton fat. This had been acquired by his Maltese clerk in some simple but dishonest manner. The damsel simpered into the conversation which afterwards was conducted by them alone.

Opportunity for proving friendship was abundant in the Red Sea and no opportunity was neglected. Lieut Hunt, who is a grandson of old Leigh Hunt [poet, d.1859. Imprisoned for libelling Prince Regent] was in six days an engaged man. He was returning to his old appointment at Madras, Miss Turner travelling to be married in Ceylon. The unexpected train of circumstances, some anxiety and previous exposure brought on a sharp attack of liver complaint and as an immediate consequence a disclosure of his love to the young lady's guardians who are of course much disgusted. The doctors say the young man should get leave to go home to recruit his health instead of thinking of matrimony. The elders say that she should fulfil her engagement. The girl says she won't. The Lieut says uncertainty causes his disease—and the by-standers watch the comedy thinking of the coffee planter now on the shore to which we are approaching, awaiting the arrival of his bride—who is really a very attractive girl, but not fully sympathetic with him, as he gained his first wife by a trick similar to that from which he is now about to suffer.

Sunday Evening

We are now off Galle light house but did not arrive till sunset and therefore cannot enter until tomorrow morning as the entrance is dangerous. We are often thinking of you and we hope soon to have news after we land in Calcutta.

The boys' holidays are now over and Julia has a quiet house again. Brickwood and Cuthbert are good friends evidently as ever and this is as it should be.

Monday

The English bound mail steamer *Simla* is now in harbour but starting soon so I despatch this. The anxious lovers came on board this morning—one returns to shore triumphant—the other loses his bride and is disappointed.

Much love from C.V. and self

Your afft brother

Alfred H. Vaux.

The previous letter was sent from Ceylon on 27 July 1868 yet it is recorded that Frederick Vaux was born in Calcutta on 26 August. It must have been touch and go whether the birth would occur at sea or on dry land, so presenting a rather harrowing quandary for poor Caroline in her first confinement. She can at best have had very few days to settle down in Calcutta before the event.

Some time that autumn—or at any rate while they were in Calcutta and before Alfred bought another horse—he wrote, probably to the children, what must have been a most amusing letter. Sadly, only the smallest scrap survives.

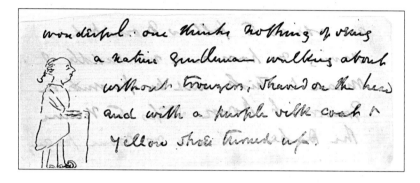

On the other side was written:

> are ordered to follow mounted. Having no horse and no saddle I mean to shirk and be present on Government House steps to receive the Duke. There is no room for . . .

In the New Year of 1869 Alfred sent two little notes to Alice. The first was written on paper headed 'Bengal Club 25 Chowringee', which was presumably in Calcutta, but it is datelined Simla with no indication of what Alfred was doing up there in mid-winter.

Simla

12 Jan. 1869

Dear little Alice,

I think that you improve in your writing and I dare say in your spelling also.

I should like to have your little hand in mind and take a

nice walk to the pond and round by the forge and past the field where we used to pick up the acorns.

On Sunday last at ¼ to five o'clock we had an earthquake here. The pond water was moved to and fro and the chandeliers hanging from the ceilings moved backwards and forwards. The floor shook and there was a rumbling noise. The church which Mama and I had been at in the morning was shaken so much that the clock stopped. We were quite uncomfortable.

> Kiss Granny for me
> Your affect father   Alfred H. Vaux.

The second note was even smaller, with no indication of where it was written—so probably Calcutta, for it was on the usual paper.

My dear little Alice,

Freddy sends his love to you and sometimes he wears frocks which once were worn by you. Please write to me another letter soon.

> Your loving father
> Alfred H. Vaux.   16 Feb 69

This little note was the more poignant in that Frederick is recorded as having died in Calcutta three weeks later, on 8 March 1869, at the age of 6½ months.

Emily Williams was always a poor correspondent and sometimes her brother had to give her a jog to extract a letter from her. This he did in August 1869. He mentions that he has been six months (i.e. since February 1869) in his present quarters—this must or may have been better accommodation in Calcutta, for he also mentions the approaching birth of Percy, who was born in the October, in Calcutta.

My dear Emily,

How very expensive must be pens ink and paper in Lincolnshire when you can only send to me a newspaper now and again. I have been six months in my present quarters and have not a letter from you.

Julia in her last written on 17 July gives me an admirable account of Cuthbert and indeed of all except Sue. Mother seems to be very well and looking forward to seeing you.

Our weather is of course Xecreble, all of us are steaming and the worse for wear. Carrie is well in health as ever she was, with good appetite for meat and soup and means to gratify it—not of the best perhaps as during the rains we have not good supplies, meat and vegetables being bad and milk difficult to procure fresh. The only fruit we can obtain is custard apples which our cook, who prides himself on his English, pronounces cussed-devils.

I think that you may believe that you may be dull in Spalding and may be so widely out as to believe that your letters will not be welcome—dispel the hallucination and do right (write). What are you thinking of doing with Cuthbert? Have any of your friends shown inclination to help him or do you intend him to try at any of the public competitions? How difficult it is first to feed one's offspring and next to give them a chance of providing their own living. My time for anxiety for Brickwood for placing him will arrive soon. George seems likely to grow up prepared for the rough and tumble of a boisterous world.

As Carrie's time draws nearer, I dread the birth of a child almost. My last three children have wrung my heart but she looks forward with much joyful anticipation.

Good bye—if you don't write I shall occasionally
Yr affect AH Vaux.   12 August 1869

NB. The last three children were:

Harold   lived 2 weeks
John   lived 1 year
Frederick   lived 6½ months

As mentioned above, Caroline's first child, Frederick, died in Calcutta on 8 March 1869—but on 20 October of the same year Percy was born, also in Calcutta. Four months later Alfred wrote to his mother—mostly about teeth.

Calcutta. 15 Feb 70.

My dear Mother,

I hope that you and the children had Valentines yesterday. Yours would take the form of ordinary letters from your absent boys and girls. I was sorry to have your account of the 14th January that Julia told you that Cuthbert was seriously unwell. I would not fall in just yet with the idea that he has any chronic complaint in view of his age and it is highly probable that the Finchley school does not suit him although the course of training is all that can be desired. Brickwood seems to be in good health and I am glad that Julia has thought seriously about his teeth. I am not sanguine as to the result but have no doubt whatever of the propriety of endeavouring to do all that is possible to place the four front teeth in a line with the lower ones. I suppose that Rymer is an excellent dentist: certainly you all have a high opinion of him and his being resident in Croydon is a great advantage: it would add much to the dear boy's comfort if he could eat as others do. I dare say the Bradbury-Coles and Brick managed to pass a happy holiday. What shall I do with him? At 14 years of age the question arises constantly and I have no shadow of an answer and you cannot help me.

I told you in my last letter about the annoyance of having my furniture seized, but it is released now and we are left in quiet possession of our own property. The publicity entailed informed Mrs Monks (née Crozier) of our address and her husband and she called a few evenings ago, looking very happy and well. [I cannot imagine why he should have had his furniture seized.]

I have had another annoyance inside my jaw. On Monday last week I was dining in company with Mr and Mrs Turnbull, who are about to leave for England again, and I had toothache which became worse. On Thursday we were dining with the Foreign Secretary at rather a grand party being assembled and I think I took cold. General Fordyce was present and complimented me on my appearance after many years of Calcutta life, and I, suffering tortures at the time smiled only but I thought he might have spoken differently if he knew what was going on among my masticators. Then came sleepless nights and days spent in stamping so on Saturday I went to the dentist who drew the offender. Afterwards he suggested that he should destroy some exposed nerves in the upper jaw and I consented but had three hours of intense agony afterwards and am scarcely recovered even now.

On Sunday came Freeth and we had a short drive as I was going to call on Mrs Parker at whose house his mess-mate was staying. The boy looked remarkably well and contented.

I do not I think write to you quite so regularly as I used but I know that our letters to Croydon are common property and that you know how we get on. I think you will be pleased with Carrie's portrait. She and her baby are both well. Miriam leaves today and we have engaged a Kentish woman as nurse, wife of a soldier recommended by Mrs Chambers: the loss of three Calcutta-born children makes me timid about Percy so

Caroline's court dress for Simla.

we engaged an English woman as nurse. Mrs Chambers is to take home Susie's watch to start next month.

Good bye my dear Mother—love to you and to my children

Yr afft son A. H. Vaux

It becomes clear, from the company he kept, that Alfred was achieving a more senior position in his sphere. Starting in 1856 as an assistant engineer under Mr Vigors at Rajmahal, he was by 1860, when he received the medallion illustrated on page 107, the 'Resident Engineer' for that length of the construction. Now, ten years later, the East India Company no more and the Railway Company brought under Government control, he had become as it were an engineering civil servant, senior enough to accompany the Government when they moved up to Simla in the hot weather. There, Caroline had to have a Court Dress for official functions at Viceregal Lodge. Rents and cost of living

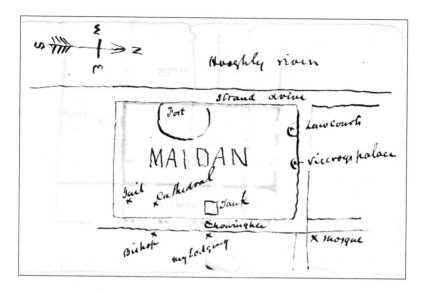

Location of Alfred's single quarters in Calcutta.

were notoriously high in Simla—Thackeray, in *Vanity Fair*, re-
marked that even Collectors could not afford to go there, preferring
Darjeeling instead. However, for Alfred there was no avoiding Simla
and in fact he left the family there for quite long periods while he
sweated it out in Calcutta. His lodgings there were on Chowringee,
where the Bengal Club was at No. 25—handy for him. This must
have cost him a lot, but we know his opinion of the Calcutta climate
for children.

From now on the letters came more from Simla than from
Calcutta.

Simla
Tuesday 3 April 1870

My dear little Alice,

Today we have been looking out for the postman expecting

that he would bring me news of my dear children from Auntie Julia, and he <u>has</u> come with a letter dated 9 April [?]. But he has not the appearance of the Croydon postman. It is the custom for the natives to take off their shoes when they come into the house so Mama, who was eager for letters, ran to the end of the verandah for them and brought mine into the little office.

I should like to see the jackdaws in the tree opening their mouths wide for food. Percy sends his love to you and informs you that he is remarkably strong and hungry every three hours, but has no teeth. He looks much better since he came to Simla and has grown quite handsome with sturdy arms and legs and such red cheeks and blue eyes— but you will be sorry to learn that he is destructive and loves to tear his nurse's hat off and when he has thrown it away he ducks down his head on her shoulder and laughs. Soon after his arrival he had a narrow escape. The bearer was carrying him down a steep hill and stumbled. Baby fell and bruised his head against a stone but the poor servant could not rise for a quarter of an hour. He very nearly broke his neck, could not straighten it for many days and was laid up to his bed for a fortnight but dear little Percy was not hurt beyond the bruise. His nurse has one boy of her own who is being taken care of by his father, a soldier, and Percy is a great favourite with her.

I don't write to Brickwood this mail but I hope he is enjoying his holiday. Give Susie a kiss from me. Tell Brick that Mr Burchell has given me a set of shirt studs, opal in the middle and small diamonds around and they look so smart that I don't know when to wear them.

Good bye my darling. I think of you every hour.
Mama sends love. Yr affect father A H Vaux.

Simla 26 May 1870

My dear Julia

Your last of the 29 April gave me accounts of the two children having whooping cough, which I was sanguine enough to think were satisfactory as they did not seem to be much pulled down—poor little darlings, I sympathise with them very much and I shall scrape a £10 note together to assist you to give them a change. So my remittance for the last quarter will be £110.5.0 and I will write to order it to be sent shortly. I am glad you received the £100/ for the third quarter all right.

I thought that dear Kate would have been upstairs before the end of April.

Yesterday Vigors came up to spend some time with us looking quite well and being glad of the change from the plains. Carrie and I on Saturday evening went to a grand reception in honour of Sir Henry Durand who is now the Lieut Gov. of the Punjab—music, conversation, ices and grand dresses were the entertainment for three hours. On Tuesday, the Queen's Birthday, was a levee at which I had to be present, a very different affair from the last—we all made our bows in a quarter of an hour.

I observe that the other under-secretaries [so now we know his grade], not military, wear the windsor uniform which is very gold and blue, sword etc, but I don't want to add cocked hat and gilded caparisons to my other expenses if I can help it. Really it makes one quite uncomfortable to ride in the middle of the day clad in a black dress coat, waistcoat and trowzers surmounted by a chimney pot hat, white gloves and white tie. I quite felt, on Tuesday, as my horse danced in the flower beds before Govt House when the salute was fired, that there was something wrong about my dress, that I had come out without my coat or with my waistcoat buttons wrong side before or something of that kind: with feathers and sword it would have been much worse.

The weather is getting hot but is pleasant in the house and likely to remain so, but my dear the B—S! Really turtles are small to them and the stars are few in comparison. Nurse intercepted a marauding party of five on the wall the other evening. They make a ruby necklace round Carrie's neck to adorn her for the party, and used to drop on my papers in my little office causing so much apprehension that I wore my hat—a capital protection. The house is built in wood in great measure and the disagreeable people have free board and lodging. Our great comfort is that other people suffer rather more than we do, besides having the fish insects a tribe which pervade the premises and destroy clothes in a night: from them we are almost free—in June we are to have sand-flies and in July fleas but we have few mosquitoes and are free from some European annoyances

such as gas, for which we have

or drains, for we have

or bursting water pipes, for we have skins

The following month there was another little letter for Alice. 'Sunnybank' was the name of the house they were renting in Simla, where everything had to be as English as possible—from roses in the gardens to log fires indoors.

Sunnybank

29 June

My dear little Alice

We have had such heavy rain that Percy can scarcely go out in the morning. At six o'clock he is very impatient and wishes to be carried over the hills but the rain has been too constant to allow him to go so he stops in the verandah looking at the men repairing this roof below the dining room. There are no tiles or slates, only clay and gravel laid on boards so of course heavy rain falls through directly and the inmates  have to beat the clay as close as they can with mallets, but they all get wet and rain comes through the sloping boards of the roof pit-pat pit-pat into the fender. We keep up a little fire in several rooms because the house is built against the rock and is damp.

The blue scarf put in the parcel which is to be posted today is for you and I hope that you will like it. I think it is made by the Kashmiri work people who live in these mountains. It is a birthday present to arrive before the right day.

Percy, Mama and I all send love to Alice. Yr afft father

Alfred H. Vaux.

Alfred wrote to his mother by the same mail as to Alice. The reference to Vigors, his first boss, is revealing—it rather looks as though Alfred had overtaken him professionally.

29 June 1870. Simla

My dear Mother,

We have been expecting all this morning that our English letters would arrive but the rain has I suppose delayed them. The rain is quite as bad here as down on the plain, indeed it has been almost incessant without a fine day for a week past. For the last ten days Carrie and I have been laid up with diarrhoea and I do not think we are much better yet. Carrie has scarcely eaten anything and I only soup and rice pudding. The baby and Vigors continue well I am most thankful to write and nurse who was ailing is better.

Since we have been up here our boxes which were stored in the Govt offices in Calcutta have been broken open and many things stolen. The thief who was one of the office people took a fancy to Carrie's wedding dress and cut up the skirt for native clothing and was discovered taking it away. Some public property was taken also and the man was punished by having two months imprisonment. We cannot yet say what has been stolen besides the white silk dress and the lace on it. We know that seven dress pieces which were locked up for safety are gone and fear that all the baby linen was stolen also. A list of the contents has been made out and we know that the loss is very great but cannot make out its extent until we return to Calcutta. Of course there is no redress. The cost of sending home money is heavy just now and the doctor coming daily to the house causes expense in other ways—but we keep up a cheerful heart over our toast and water.

We are invited to dine at Lord Napier's on Monday, but I do not think we can go, which will disappoint Carrie.

Vigors still stays with us and does not seem to be nearer obtaining an appointment than when he came up. Our last from you contained Calvert's letter from Chicago, which I was glad to have, and also the news that you and the babes were better.

Good bye—best love. Yr afft Son Alfred H. Vaux.

And again, by the mail a month later—Vigors still staying with them!

Simla 29 July 1870

My dear Mother,

I was very glad to have your letter dated the 1st July and to hear your gossip—perhaps by this time you may have been allowed to see the new grandchild Mabel and to congratulate Kate on her more roomy abode.

My little office upstairs [must have been a study] is just seven feet square, and even into this small space the boots intrude under the curtain from the dressing room, but I find that a large space is not necessary if one wants to work.

 A frightful gun which is situated 100 feet above our chimneys has just startled me and told me that it is noon. One is never prepared for the report and I am frightened out of my chair, also out of my wits, daily by the explosion which reverberates round the distant hills as if they also resented the noise.

We live for the most part in fog and I have a fire generally in three rooms out of the four, not because it is cold but because the damp is disagreeable.

When the cloud lifts we have beautiful peeps of scenery and the constant rain makes the different greens of fern, cedar, pine and moss to be charming. Our view at the back of the house is as I before described limited to a rough lichen covered rock a few feet away. On two sides, East and West, we have near hills and to the South rises Tarn Davy, a magnificent mountain, and to the south west a break in the hills admits us to see the plain of Hindoostan and the Sutlej river rolling as a bright streak towards the Indus and the Indian Ocean: the river where we see it must be 35 miles off and the verge of the horizon just 100 miles. Although Loodiana and other large cities are within the scope of our vision we can make out nothing and the vast plain looks like a sea. Often we enjoy a clear atmosphere up here and look over the plains below on which there roll patches of cloud. The dark grey surface of the plains resembles the ocean and the fleecy clouds look like surf beating on the shore or on half covered rocks.

Although the scenery is certainly very fine and the air cool (67° in the verandah) I do not consider the climate at this season to be healthy. Vigors, baby and nurse are in excellent case and Carrie fairly but I still suffer and many others around equally and in the same manner. Bismuth was not found to answer so I am now taking every four hours a pill composed of lead and ipecacuanha. There is really a great deal of illness and I think that the delicious soft air and much else that is written of Simla an exaggeration. Lord Mayo [the Viceroy] hates the place but I should enjoy the scenery, the walks and the temperatures thoroughly if I were not troubled by the disorder which has continued for the last six weeks.

One of my servants has been behaving badly in drinking my wine. I brought up three dozen of brandy to last the seven months and find that two dozen have been drunk by him and this represents in Simla nearly £9. Beer and wine have also been consumed largely but I do not know to what extent exactly. To balance this dishonesty another servant last Sunday brought me a packet of Govt Telegraph labels which he had found on the road. According to the modern system Telegraph messages are stamped like letters instead of being prepaid, and these stamps some of which are worth £2 and £3 had been dropped: in all the value of the labels amounted to £53.10.0, but a claimant in the shape of a native Treasury clerk soon appeared and the property for which he was responsible was restored on the payment of a reward to the finder of twenty five rupees.

I am so glad that you enjoyed your visit to Dr Bowerbank and that Susie was good. I read all about the microscope meeting in the *C. Chronicle.* Good bye, much love.

Yr afft Son Alfred H. Vaux.

The letter illustrated overleaf is one of the few we have from Caroline Vaux. It is clearly written in Simla but is undated. However, as Percy's birthday on 20 October is mentioned as a recent occurrence and Charles, who was born in February 1871, is *not* mentioned, it should be safe to date the letter late October 1870. Caroline's round and generous writing is far easier to read than was Em's spidery hand, but it is amusing that she has no use for commas and full stops. It is quite clear where they were meant to go in, but she apparently would not waste ink on the things.

Although the last letter was dated October 1870 we have no more until March 1872. The intervening 17 months had however not been uneventful.

In October or November 1870 the family, as Caroline had forecast, moved down to Calcutta. Here on 27 February 1871, was born Charles Alfred Vaux who was to become father of John and

My dear Alice

By the time you get this we shall I hope be in Calcutta Percy is looking forward with great delight to the journey but it is rather a troublesome one for Papa & me I [am sure] you would enjoy it very much It is so cold here we don't know how to keep ourselves warm & I am sitting now close to the fire there is a hard frost every night which is unusual at this time of year We had a great treat for Percy on his birthday We screened off part of the room & lighted it up to make

a little theatre and then had an entertainment of dancing dolls There is a man here who is very clever with them A good many children came to spend the afternoon and they all enjoyed themselves very much After the theatricals were over they all played a little while in the garden and then came in to tea after which as it was getting dark they all went home You don't very often write to us but we are always glad to get a letter Give our love to Grannie and kind regards to Miss Bell

Believe me ever dear Alice
Yours affec'ately
Caroline Vaux.

Peter Vaux and thus, alone of Alfred's children, responsible for continuing the name of the family in the male line. His parents and brothers and sisters always called him Charlie.

Tragically for everyone, however, on 1 September of that year, 1871, Julia died at the age of forty-one. This must have been a terrible loss, for not only was she a special favourite of Alfred's (his spirits always rose when he sat down to write to her) but she must have been the lynch-pin at Canterbury Road. Mother was now seventy-eight. Both married daughters had moved away; Calvert was in America and Julia seems to have been keeping house—it was she, for instance, to whom Alfred sent his quarterly allowance for the children. Mother, of course, could not care for them all by herself and so, during 1872, we find them becoming scattered. Brickwood (sixteen) seems to have joined his Aunt Emily and Cuthbert in Lincolnshire while Sue (fourteen) went to her god-mother, also Susan Vaux, in Teignmouth. It seems possible that George (ten) and Alice (nine) stayed on with their Grannie.

1 March 72

My dear Susie,

You will be pleased I think to know that Auntie Kate and I are trying to arrange that you should go to school at Mid-summer.

You are such a great girl now that I am sure you ought to be learning. [There had of course been the governess, Miss Bell.] My dear Cousin Susan at Teignmouth is interesting herself about you and I hope that we shall be able to find a good school.

Give my love to my little Alice and a kiss also. Percy and Charles are quite well and happy.

Your affect father Alfred H Vaux.

As always in Alfred's family, children continued to arrive regularly each year, so that it is no surprise to learn that, despite Charlie's birth in February 1871, another boy is two weeks old in March the following year. At least one can say that they seemed always to be most welcome and their loss deeply felt. However, by now Carrie and the boys are back in Simla—but in a different house from the last one. I have inserted Carrie's commas for her.

Oakley Lodge
March 26 1872

My dear Susie,

The pinafore you made for your little brothers arrived quite safely and I was delighted with it. It is very handsome and fits Charlie beautifully so I shall keep it for a going out pinafore as it is too good to wear in common. You must thank Alice for it too as I don't know which of you made it, but it is very nice.

Your 3rd little brother is a fortnight old and such a big boy; he is already quite a weight to carry about. I think the fine Simla air agrees well with him. Percy was not at all pleased with him at first and said if the nurse had brought him she might take him away again for he did not want him. I wish it had been a little sister for him, it would have been much nicer. I do not know what we shall call him yet. What do you think about Leonard or Hugh? Papa suggests nothing but James which is a name I cannot bear. I must wait till he comes up before we decide. [Clearly this child had been born in Simla, not Calcutta.]

I do not expect to see him for another five weeks, about the 1st of May. I hope it will not be later than that as we are both quite tired of living alone. He will have a terribly hot journey up but I hope the mountain air will revive him.

I often think how pleased you would be with Percy if you could see him. He is such a clever child, and now he has grown quite good. He and Charlie have white flannelled frocks and jackets trimmed with bands of scarlet and straw hats, and they look so sweet in them. Little Charlie trots about all over the house now and thinks himself quite a man.

The hills are covered with crimson rhododendrons in full bloom. I can only see them through the window as I am not able to go out yet, but I hope in two or three days I shall get out for an hour in the Dandy. The air is so delicious, the cold weather is quite gone now. We have given up fires and have doors and windows all open. The children play in the garden all day only coming in to eat and sleep. They are out walking every morning at ½ past 7 and come in about ½ past 9 as after that the sun gets too hot.

I wonder how you will like going to school—I should fancy very much. I hope you manage to be a little while with your brother and Alice during the holidays. In another three years you will be thinking of coming out to us. I hope we shall still be in Simla, it is such a delightful place and I am sure you would like it. It is still very empty but I daresay next month it will begin to fill. Papa complains of the great heat in Calcutta both night and day; old Indians who have been out here for years say they never remember such heat at this time of year.

I must say good bye for today.
With much love to all
Believe me dear Suzie
Ever yours affect'ately
Caroline Vaux.

Calcutta

2 May 1872

My dear Susie,

I was surprised and pleased to hear last Monday when the English letters arrived that you were expecting to go to school immediately. It is kind of Aunt Susan to take charge of you and I think that you will be quite happy. You must ask Aunt Susan how you will arrange about writing to me as I shall like to know how you get on. Perhaps a letter once monthly will be enough and I hope to hear that you are growing bodily and mentally into an upright little woman.

I hear every day from Mama who with her three little boys is enjoying most delightful weather at Simla.

Percy is growing old enough to know how to behave himself but Charlie is a sadly passionate little fellow.

Tomorrow the third of May we expect our new Governor General to arrive and soon after he has taken his oath I hope that we shall be ordered out of Calcutta.

Good bye—my little Sue. Remember your loving father

Alfred H Vaux.

Horse-drawn Gharry.

The above was found tucked into a letter which had been written in Calcutta. It must have been sketched in the city, because in

Simla no one but the Viceroy, the Governor of the Punjab and the Commander in Chief might use a carriage. For others there were rickshaws. The 'Dandy' mentioned by Caroline a couple of letters back is described in the encyclopaedia as: '(Anglo-Ind.) Strong cloth hammock slung from pole, carried shoulder-high by two or more men (common means of transport in hilly districts).'

Alfred did not arrive in Simla by 1 May as his wife had hoped, but he was there by the 26th when the latest little boy was christened. On the following day both parents wrote to the girls at home. Sue of course was at school at Teignmouth—she certainly did not lack for the sort of fatherly advice which no fourteen-year-old would swallow today.

> Simla
> 27 May 1872

My dear Susie,

I have your letter of the 18 April. It was received this morning and too late for Mama and me to consider whether your youngest brother should be christened by either of the names you have proposed, Herbert or Arthur. Yesterday at Christchurch he was baptised after the evening service and received the names Edmund Julian. He will be called Edmund and the other name is introduced in remembrance of my loved sister your dear Aunt Julia, who was so kind to you and to whom we owe so much.

I like to hear of your masters and mistresses and expect to soon hear that my little Sue is an accomplished good girl. If I were you I should have a sheet of paper in my portfolio and I would write a few words to papa frequently. Then on Saturday when you have spare time you can make up the letter. Your own dear mother was so good a musician that I think you ought to inherit some of her talent. 'Fräulein' insists

167

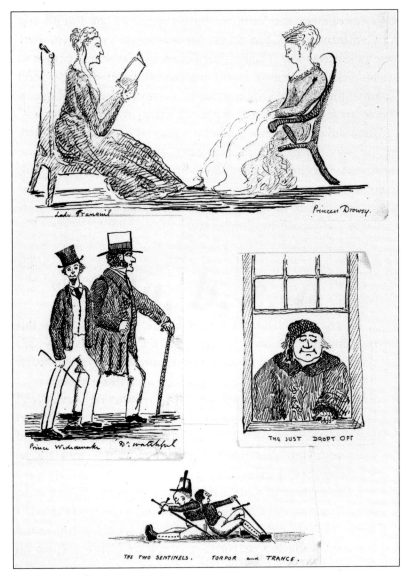

Caroline liked to keep in touch with Alice and Susan by writing them children's stories,
which Alfred would illustrate.
These are from 'Prince Wideawake's Adventures in the Land of Nod'.

168

on careful fingering and upright attitudes and I am sure you will be attentive. Discipline is the right thing Susie, discipline makes the soldier and the school girl also.

You would have been pleased to see Percy in church yesterday. He looked and behaved quite well but I am afraid that he has not that full regard for the nature of discipline that he should have. Mama and he send their love with mine.

Your affectionate father
Alfred H Vaux.

The following extract is from Dennis Kincaid's *British Social Life in India*—from which I have cribbed various remarks which I have occasionally inserted:

> 'At the top of the Mall rises Christchurch's noble Gothic structure. It was as certain a rendezvous on Sunday morning as any church on the plains. But they emerged more sedately from under the Tudor porch with its crenellated roof. Topis were hardly necessary, and though some of the gentlemen wore those odd honeycomb-shaped topis others preferred less tropical headgear. None of the ladies wore topis. Here at last they could sport their wide-brimmed straw hats with banks of flowers and ostrich feathers; and it was comforting to be able to wear a feather boa without feeling too hot. There was no veranda here, for everything about Christchurch had to be as English as possible. You came out on to a little terrace with a fence round it and a wide view over Simla. There was of course no parade of carriages.'

It must have seemed very different from the little church at

Monghyr, where George and Alice had been christened and where Alfred had had to ginger up the padre.

Anyway, Caroline's description of the ceremony was rather different to her husband's.

Oakley Lodge
May 27th

My dear Alice,

As Papa is writing to Sue I must send you a line. I don't know whether when you receive this you will be still at Croydon or not, but you seem to be tolerably happy wherever you are which is a great blessing.

Your 3rd little Indian brother was christened yesterday Edmund Julian. He behaved beautifully and was wide awake all the time. Percy looked charming in a white frock with rose-coloured trimmings and a grey felt hat. He was quite quiet until he saw some brass headed nails in the next pew, when he began '1 2 3 4 5 I caught a hare alive' but after he was stopped at that amusement was perfectly good for the rest of the time. I did not take Charlie as I thought he would cry.

Tell dear Granny I got her letter this morning and was so pleased that she seemed well and cheerful. Papa was not well after he first came up but is all right again now. He has just gone off to office on his pony and I shall go down and fetch him about 5 o'clock when we take a nice walk. The babies all go out with us together.

Good bye for today
Much love from your affec'ate
Caroline Vaux.

22 July 1872

My dear little Alice,

I have your letter of the 12 June telling me of the kind Mrs
Purdie's present of a doll and I trust that her character for
amiability, tidiness and amenability to discipline will prove as
satisfactory as that of your other dolls and that you will not be
troubled by any perversity of disposition. How sad if, after all
your care, she should become quarrelsome.

Charlie does not care much for dolls but derives amusement
from bringing croquet mallets frequently on to the dolls' noses.
Percy and Charles both love to be out of doors hammering
and digging and watching the actions of the servants so that
they may imitate them.

On Saturday Mama and I went up to the top of the high
mountain which is behind the house for the first time this year
and we saw the old hermit, who has improved his house. It
is surrounded by the monkeys who are fed by him and who
gather round the place in the evening. They seemed to be
enjoying themselves thoroughly, swinging from one cedar tree
to another and poking their red faces round the stems to look
at, and disapprove, of us. The chief monkey is called Rajah
and is an extremely noble personage.

I should like to have you with me to take walks together
but Croydon is a much nicer place and I am sure that you are
happier than you would be if you lived with me. Grannie tells
me that you know the Blue Bells of Scotland and I expect
soon to hear that you know several airs—and that you practise
scales regularly.

Good bye my dear. Love from Mama and the little boys.

Your affectionate father   Alfred H Vaux

4 August 1872

My dear Susie,

Your letter written from Teignmouth pleases me, and Aunt Susan wrote such loving words about you that I felt grateful to her. Now I suppose that you are at Croydon, soon to return to school and to start work again. I am interested in the school work and shall like to know what you like best, history or French or music—also I want to know the sequel of those trials to swim, for every girl as well as boy ought to be able to swim.

Today I feel very tired as Mama and I were watching little Edmund last night. He is suffering from a very bad cough and, poor little fellow, can only sleep for a few minutes at a time. At five o'clock this morning, before the sun had risen, I saw a beautiful rainbow larger than the half arch, but the cloud and fog have come down over the hills again and we have heavy rain.

Good bye Susie—I notice that you try to be a good brave girl—and love you for it.

Your affect father   Alfred H Vaux.

And so the little monthly notes to the children continued, but only the girls kept theirs, so we do not know what was said to the boys.

Simla
15 Sept 72

My dear little Alice,

According to promise a parcel of sweets has gone to Mary and I hope that they will meet with the approval of that young lady. Toys from Benares should have accompanied but by accident they were left behind owing to Mr Bayne not having been able to procure them. These wooden toys must therefore be despatched hereafter. They are fitted only for the younger children and not for ladies who are as old as you and Mary.

Mama sends her love to you. She was with a party of ladies and gentlemen yesterday in the valley near Simla and had to pass along the bed of the river in order to see a beautiful cavern into which the water falls and, as some of the rocks were too wide apart to allow of the people jumping from one to another, attendants carried a plank. Unfortunately one of the gentlemen was very portly, and when the journey was half performed his weight broke the plank so the poor ladies had to wade for the rest of the way and were all wet through. Wasn't it fun?

Good bye my dear. Ever your loving father Alfred H Vaux

25 Oct 1872

My dear little Alice,

I wish that you could see your dear little brothers in Simla, with their red faces and sturdy limbs, trotting up and down the hills in their long great coats on the frosty mornings.

Percy and Charlie can run about very briskly but little Edmund cannot of course walk as he is only seven months old. Every thing that others do the two eldest must attempt— they spend part of Monday in writing out the list of clothes for the washerman and regularly in the afternoon they go with Mama to the wood house to assist in cutting up the fuel. The children are rather small for their age but exceedingly active, both in their legs and tongues. Percy is chattering all day long—Charlie cannot talk yet but is none the quieter—he promises to produce a bass voice of great power after a few years and will be able to accompany you when you are a middle aged woman. They both send their love to you. [Charlie certainly never sang!]

Mind that you take care of Grannie now that you have so much to do with her, and, whenever you like, write a letter to me to tell all the Canterbury Road news.

Good bye now—accept much love from your affectionate father   Alfred H Vaux.

Simla

4 November 1872

My dear Susie,

I have your letter of the 6 October and send to you Mama's and my love. We are glad to hear that one of your schoolfellows was allowed to be with you during your holidays and would have liked to hear her name.

Now that you are at school and are really a great girl I expect to have a good account of your progress in study and at your work. So much of your happiness in afterlife will depend upon your industry now that I trust you will do your best. Unless young ladies can be useful in many ways they are apt to be put on one side and they cannot learn to be useful without applying their minds and being persevering.

Mama is very useful in Simla as a visiting lady under the Committee of the Mayo Memorial School and takes charge of the clothing of the girls and boys. She is an excellent needle-woman owing to her industry when she was a girl and now her knowledge is turned to good account, not in working herself for the children but in helping others work and in making purchases. When she was a girl also Mama learnt to sing glees by constantly practising, and you would be quite glad to see how useful she is in the Church Choir as she keeps all the ladies right, on one side of the church, by singing correctly. There are many young ladies in Simla who are unable to do any thing really well and they don't seem to make friends. They appear to be out of place and I often think to myself—is that the kind of girl that my Sue will be?—and I always answer No.

We are packing up—four mules' burden, four men's burden to go with us down the hills. Carts and camels have taken much heavy baggage beforehand.

Good bye my Susie—much love from your father

Alfred H Vaux.

And so, during the month of November, they all went down to the plains again and returned to the steamy heat of Calcutta. It comes as no surprise to find that poor little Edmund died as soon as they arrived—on 5 December 1872. Born 9 months previously in Simla, where he had thrived so well on the mountain air, Calcutta did for him—as it had already taken two of Alfred's children. At first sight it seems strange that in none of the letters we have does Alfred mention the loss of a child. On the contrary, a gap in the correspondence always follows such an event. He was, however, so very fond of his children that his mother may have thought those letters too harrowing to keep.

Such a gap occurred on this occasion, so that they are all back again in Simla before we have the next letter. Percy helped his father write to Alice who, nearly eleven, was possibly staying with Kate and going to school with one of her 'chicks'.

Simla 22 May 1873

My dear Alice,

I send my love to you. Yesterday Percy and Mama, with Charlie and two young friends, named Molesworth, went out in the afternoon to Armondale to have tea in the open air under the cedar trees. Charlie collected the wood for the fire while Percy and his young friends amused themselves by throwing stones into a pool of water. They enjoyed themselves very much and came up the steep hill at eight o'clock.

Both your little brothers are unusually strong on their legs and you would be pleased to see them skipping from the rocks like little kids. I really think that they would beat you in a race up and down hill.

Mary Withers and you will be happy companions in the school room and pleasant playground at Streatham but you will be sorry to lose your kind Miss Bell.

Good bye my little Alice. Mama sends love—with me

Your affect father Alfred H Vaux.

Now, with father guiding the hand holding the pen, Percy had a go.

My dear Sister,

I should like you to gather flowers with me. I love my sister and would like her so much in this room. I have got a wheel barrow and I would like you to put sand in it and throw it down the *khud*. I should like you to make snowballs with me. I have got a nurse called Mary.

Good bye,

Your loving brother Percy

The next time Percy communicated with Alice he got his nurse Mary to write the letter for him. This was not really in her line but they managed. Like her mistress, Mary had no use for punctuation.

My dear Alice

I love my Alice and I should like her to come in this room I send a kiss to my sister I and Charlie are going up to the top of a big hill 2 have tea

I should like you to play hide and seek with me I should like to show you the lions and tigers at Barrackpore and the big snake that spit at me

I have been to a big party at the Lord Sahibs

your loving brother

Percy Vaux

Dear Alice

Percy has been writing you a letter all his own dictation to Nurse Mary Papa is too busy to write today Give our love to Grannie and tell her we are all quite well We have lovely weather now but expect the rains in another week Percy wears a sailor suit now and goes to church so you see he is getting quite a big boy Good bye dear child for today

Your loving Caroline Vaux

There are now only three more letters left in the box, all being written by Alfred to Susan. But they tell a story.

Simla 26 May 73

My dear Susie,

I was so sorry to hear from your last letter that you were suffering from the toothache—one large friend, turned into an enemy, had been removed.

What a big girl my little Sue must be if she is 5' 3" in height—why Aunt Susan herself is scarcely more than that.

I should like to hear the Perle du Nord and hope to do so someday but I cannot yet name that day my dear. You have asked for photographs of Charlie and Percy but I fear that we shall not be able to send them for photography is so very expensive in India. They are active rosy little fellows, quite mountaineers and Mary their Nurse has difficulty in preventing them from climbing the trees. Percy can say several hymns and speaks English nicely, but Charlie is not so forward except in Hindoostani.

> Good bye Sue. Much love from Mama and your
> affect father   Alfred H Vaux.

Simla 28 July 1873

My dear Sue,

I have been thinking of your birthday and congratulate you on being 15 years old. I suppose that you spent last Friday in the new house at Streatham with Alice and Grandmama and that you are now again at Heavitree. Mama and I remember Brian and Janet Hamilton quite well, for they lived close to Oakley Lodge at the top of the hill.

Charlie and Percy send their love to you but have difficulty in understanding about their English sisters.

Mind you tell me what you think of Alice—whether she is grown or not. Your loving father

Alfred H Vaux.

The last letter of all, at the bottom of the box, is in a little envelope of its own, bearing the imprint of an Exeter stationer. Pencilled on it in a round girlish hand are the words 'Papa's last letter'. The letter within it is very well-worn and the ink faded while the writing itself betrays the familiar shakiness of fever.

Simla 8 Sept 1873

My dear Susie,

I was glad to receive your note from Streatham telling me of your impressions on seeing brothers and sister after a long absence, and Aunt Emily has written describing your happy visit to Spalding. This must have been an agreeable change indeed. The companionship of the nice young ladies, the garden and that dear pony made up I would think all that could be desired.

But you will not have been disinclined to return to your good friends the Misses Irvines at Heavitree [this must be the school at Teignmouth]. Aunt Susan writes to me regularly and tells how you grow and such other news as I desire concerning you. I am most grateful to her for the kind solicitude with which she watches over your welfare. You do not yet know how unhappy is a young girl's lot who has no mother, and who does not find a good Aunt Susan to look after her, but I am sure you know how to be grateful for affection.

I think that you love your dear old father and I expect that you will love Aunt Susan also who takes papa's place and who loves you dearly. I am now looking at the photograph which came last night and shows my Sue with a brother on each side and looking over Alice's head and I am much pleased with the group. Your face seems to be in much better focus than Alice's but I recognise the excellent likenesses of three, George, Sue and Alice. Alfred [he has always been Brickwood before] seems to be such a great fellow that I scarcely make out the features of the boy I left in England in 1868.

Do you remember that certain gold Delhi crosses were posted and lost years ago? Mama and I chose two more a few days ago and I have sent them in a registered letter to Aunt Susan. There is one for you and another for Alice—they are simple and I think very pretty—tell me if that is your opinion also when the present arrives, which of course may not be till you again go to Teignmouth.

You have asked me for a photograph of myself but I have not been to the shop for years and have no picture later than that which you have and which is still very like me.

179

Percy and Charles send their love and so does Mama.

                      Good bye—Your affect father   Alfred
                      H Vaux

'The last good bye' is pencilled in that girlish hand.

There is an unusual and perhaps prophetic melancholy in the above, for Alfred died in Simla on 16 October 1873. That was possibly even before Susan received this letter. The cause of death was cholera and, as the announcement indicates, it came suddenly.

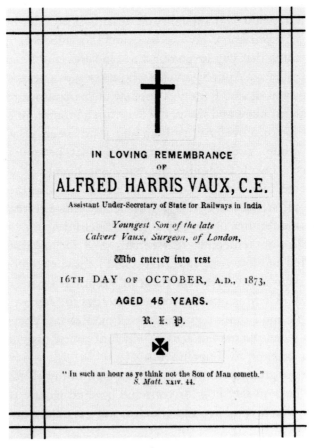

IN LOVING REMEMBRANCE
OF
ALFRED HARRIS VAUX, C.E.
Assistant Under-Secretary of State for Railways in India

Youngest Son of the late
Calvert Vaux, Surgeon, of London,

𝕿𝖍𝖔 𝖊𝖓𝖙𝖊𝖗𝖊𝖉 𝖎𝖓𝖙𝖔 𝖗𝖊𝖘𝖙

16TH DAY OF OCTOBER, A.D., 1873,

AGED 45 YEARS.

R. I. P.

" In such an hour as ye think not the Son of Man cometh."
S. Matt. xxiv. 44.

In the late summer of 1873 there was an outbreak of cholera which, owing to a failure to separate the stricken from the still healthy, had by October developed into an epidemic. Alfred, who clearly understood the urgent need for isolation of the cholera victims, personally took charge of an operation to enforce this and thereby saved countless lives. No doubt he made use of the railway to do so. However, in the process he caught cholera himself and died very quickly.

At forty-five Alfred had died young even by the standards of nineteenth-century India, so that it is interesting to speculate what position he would have reached had he lived to retirement age. One wonders too how many children he might have fathered by then. He had at any rate achieved the grade of Chief Engineer which Emily, his first wife, had been convinced his health would never permit. His children held divided opinions about the matter. The four orphans of 'Em' and Alfred held that the latter's death was heroic and brought up the then unborn baby Julian and his daughter Margaret to believe this. Percy and Charlie, who saw their mother left in the lurch, felt that his first duty should have been to her and her children rather than risking his life on behalf of 'the natives'. There are usually two points of view about anything—'Carrie' may well have supported the first.

Caroline, pregnant once more, was indeed left in an awkward situation, for she must have felt it essential to get home before March 1874, when her next child was due; she must sail from Calcutta at the latest by Christmas, and it was already late October. Before leaving Simla she had not only to book the family passages and arrange to return the nurse Mary to her husband, but also to dispose of the contents of her house—just when everyone was packing up to leave for the Plains—and on arrival in Calcutta to deal with the family effects in store there.

She would have had another and more serious worry. Alfred

Mrs Caroline Vaux aged about 65.

had always been doubtful about what pensions the East India Company and later the Indian Government would provide for widows. He himself had had eighteen years' service almost to the day since he first sailed from England, but that would not have qualified him for the maximum pension. Caroline had been married to him for only six of those years. In fact she did receive some sort of pension, but it would probably have been small and slow to come through.

However, she and the two little boys of just four and almost three did get home in time, speeded by the existence of the Suez Canal, which had been opened four years previously. As she passed between the banks cut into the desert sand she may have reflected how very interested Alfred would have been to see this engineering marvel.

Her fifth son (the third to survive) was born in Richmond, Surrey, on 13 March 1874 and christened Alfred Julian—two years and a day after the birth of poor Edmund Julian. It was said that they were each given the name of Julian because, like Julius Caesar, they were born in the Ides of March. But Alfred had also said that he wished to remember his sister Julia.

Alfred Brickwood Vaux, aged seventeen and now called Alfred, had become the head of the family, the duties of which position he was to discharge faithfully until he died at the age of ninety-two. His first task was to help his step-mother deal with his father's will. Extracts from this are on the following pages and include a copy of Alfred's summary of the residual estate. This, if nothing else, provides convincing proof that Alfred Harris Vaux, as a loyal and honest servant of the country to which he had devoted his life's work, took from it no more than his just and modest due.

WILL OF ALFRED HARRIS VAUX

This is the last Will and Testament of me Alfred Harris Vaux of Calcutta, Civil Engineer.

[Now follows a long legal description of what the estate might consist of in the way of property, money, debts due and owed, etc before coming to the nub of the matter]

. . . unto my children, my Wife and my sister Julia Desborough Vaux in equal portions to and for their own use and benefit absolutely. And I nominate, constitute and appoint my Wife Caroline Vaux and my sister Julia Desborough Vaux to be Executrixes of this my Will and hereby revoking all former or other Wills . . .

(Sd) Alfred Harris Vaux   Witness . . . . . .

2nd April 1869   Witness . . . . . .

I, J. W. Macnabb, Judge of the District of Simla hereby make known that on the seventh day of November in the year 1873 the last Will of Alfred Harris Vaux, late of Simla, a copy whereof is hereunto annexed was proved before me and that administration of the property and assets of the said deceased and in any way concerning his Will was granted to Caroline Vaux and sole surviving Executrix in the said Will named she having undertaken to administer the same and to make a true inventory of the said property and assets and to exhibit the same at or before the expiration of a year next ensuing and also to render a true account thereof.

(sd) J. R. Macnabb.   Judge of the District of Simla

A true copy. A. S. Gaspar.   Asst Registrar

Probate to
English Estate
granted 22nd May 1874

[As instructed, a true account was produced and a copy of this is attached.]

Copy of Extract from "Residuary Account"

On account of the personal Estate, & of moneys arising out of the estate of Alfred Harris Vaux who died on the 16th day of Oct: 1873

Description of Property

Life Assurance Policies (not yet paid)	885
Bonds Bills, Notes, & Interest due at death	10
Indian assets there converted July 1874.	700. 11. 7
	1595 : 11 : 7
Payments Fees £7:6:6. Stamp £22 Labs + cn £ 1	30 : 6 : 0
£	1565 : 5 : 7

I declare &c &c

Sd Caroline Vaux

19th August. 1874.

Note. A further small sum is expected to be received from India & on the winding up of the European Assurance Society when a further Acct will be delivered.

(Copy by A.B.V. 7th Nov—77)

185

Epilogue

WHAT BECAME OF THEM ALL

Mother

Alfred's mother was eighty-one when Caroline and the boys returned to England. She died in 1881 at the age of eighty-nine, having been a refuge and support to her children and grandchildren for nearly fifty years since her husband died.

Brothers and Sisters

Calvert Vaux did well as an architect in USA. Before his death in 1895, aged seventy-one, he had assisted in planning and laying out the grounds of the Capitol Building and the Smithsonion Institute in Washington, DC. He was also responsible for designing and constructing Central Park, New York, and parks in Brooklyn, Chicago and Buffalo. He had two sons and two daughters. The former remained bachelors, but the girls both married professors at Yale University, Donaldson and Hendrickson respectively. Their descendants still live in New England.

Emily Williams' son *Cuthbert* was well known to his cousins, especially Charlie, but the family contact faded and it is not known when mother or son died.

James Vaux died in New Zealand, but no more is known about him. He was said to have been ship-wrecked.

Julia Vaux of course died in 1871.

Mrs Emily Vaux (née Brickwood).
'Mother' in old age.

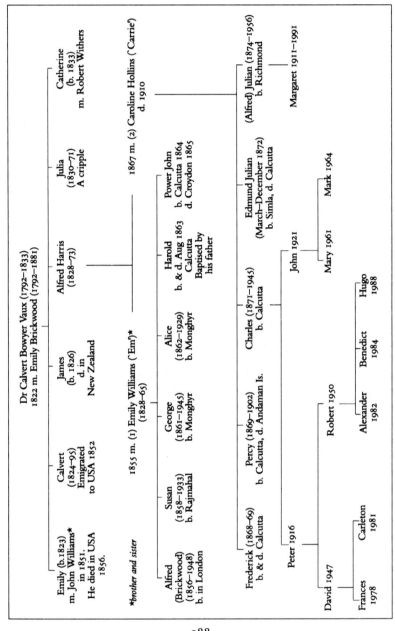

Catherine Withers ('Kate') eventually had nine 'chicks' (five girls and four boys) but this contact also faded.

Children of the First Family

Alfred Brickwood Vaux (originally 'Brickwood', later 'Alfred') took his position as head of the family seriously, being always a support and help to the others. He was a most satisfactory godfather to myself and it was he who preserved these and many other papers. He went into the India Office where he served in London—never visiting India—until his retirement about 1921. Although archaically described in the List as 'Clerk' he became in fact sufficiently senior to be allowed living quarters in the India Office Building. He received the MVO for services in connection with the visit of the Maharajah of Patiala to King George V. He died in 1948, at the age of ninety-two.

Susan Emily Vaux died in 1933, aged seventy-five. She had had a successful career as a nurse, becoming Matron of Birmingham Eye Hospital before running her own Nursing Home at Woodbridge.

George Crozier Vaux had a career in the Board of Trade. In June 1914 he represented the Board at an enquiry in Canada into the loss by collision of the CPR liner *Empress of Ireland*. After retirement he became a great grower of hybrid apples, achieving one tree with seven different varieties of fruit which survived until 1984. He died in 1945, when he was eighty-four.

Alice Eliza Vaux died in 1929, aged sixty-seven. During World War I she was in the Women's Land Army where she wore breeches, considered very advanced for the times. After the War she lived with Alfred and George in Chelsea and occupied herself in voluntary work in the East End of London. She always seemed to me, however, to disapprove of small boys.

Wife and Children of the Second Family

Caroline Vaux, although she too lost two children, did not have to endure the rugged conditions of life in rural India which undoubtedly hastened the early death of Emily, for she spent much of her time in Simla. Alfred, who so disapproved of the Calcutta climate for children, could afford to keep his family up there because he had by then become better off financially, though he was never wealthy. Caroline's ordeal came after his death, when she had three little boys to bring up on a minimum income. She managed well. For a while she ran a small school in Weymouth, but in due course moved to a house at Tonbridge. Here she was able to take advantage of the favourable terms offered by the public school to parents living within the Parish Boundary. All three boys went to Tonbridge School, but Julian was not happy there and moved on to Dulwich College. She died in 1910—we do not know at what age—having launched all her sons on their chosen careers.

Percy Vaux went into the Burma Police where he was doing well until in 1902, at the age of thirty-two, he was killed by savages in the Andaman Islands. His half-brother Alfred, at the India Office, had by chance the sad task of decoding the cable reporting the casualty. There exist full details of this sorry episode which became a *cause célèbre* at the time, because of the disgraceful circumstances in which the authorities had put his life at risk. He was unmarried and never had UK leave.

Charles Alfred Vaux (Charlie) achieved his boyhood ambition to become an explorer. He qualified as a mining engineer and led geological expeditions in East and West Africa, Siberia, the Caucasus, Manchuria and Malaya, also travelling widely elsewhere. He had creditable active service in Tunnelling Companies in France in 1914–18—and by so doing sacrificed a lucrative professional consultancy in the Far East. In 1916 he married Winifred Pryce and had two sons, details of whose families are shown in the tree. He died in 1945, aged seventy-four.

Alfred Julian Vaux (Julian) became a solicitor, practising in Croydon. He served with the Royal Berkshire Regiment in France during the Great War and then returned to the law. In 1911 he married Mabel Fenn and had one daughter, who never married. He died in 1956, aged eighty-two.

It will be seen that the eldest son of Alfred Harris Vaux was born in 1856 and the youngest died exactly one hundred years later.

POSTSCRIPT

I N October 1983 my wife and I found ourselves in New Delhi. On a balmy Sunday afternoon we hired one of those exhilarating three-wheeled taxis based upon a Harley-Davidson motor-cycle and asked to be taken to the Rail Transport Museum at Chanaka-puri on the outskirts of the city. This is said to be the best museum in India. Whether or not this is so, it is probably the finest railway museum in the world, for here are to be seen exhibits ranging from the East Indian Railway's No. 22 (*Fairy Queen*) built in 1855 and said to be the oldest working locomotive in the world, to the monster 161-ton 2–8–2 XG/M–911 (built in Manchester in 1928); special trains built for Maharajas, the Prince of Wales and the Viceroy; armoured trains; part of the rack and pinion Nilgiri Mountain Railway; a 1907 monorail and much else of fascinating interest to the enthusiast. There is also a large indoor display of maps, engineering drawings and working and scale models.

The ten-acre open display area may be toured in a charming miniature train drawn by a little steam locomotive built by ap-prentices. This being a Sunday afternoon, there was a fair crowd of Indian families, some of whom had arrived on the family motor-scooter, father riding with great care, mother and perhaps two chil-dren holding on for dear life, all in their Sunday best, silken saris billowing in the breeze. Amongst this friendly and well-behaved throng we must have been noticeably the only two white faces for, as we stepped out of the train, we were accosted by a silver-haired

Fairy Queen, *oldest working locomotive in the world.*
Built 1855 by Kitson, Thompson & Hewitson of Leeds. Valve gear by George
Stephenson. Worked mail train, East Indian Railway, from Howrah (Calcutta) to
Ragiganj (Rajmahal and Monghyr) covering 121 miles in 5 hours, from 1855–1909. Now
in New Delhi Railway Transport Museum.

gentleman who introduced himself as the curator of the museum, enquiring what could be our interest in Indian trains. When I explained that my grandfather had worked on the construction of the East Indian Railway and had been Chief Engineer of the Company in 1873 his face lit up. He took us into the indoor display building and there, on a large wall-map illuminated by coloured bulbs, he explained how and when the various sections of the EIR had been built.

When he had finished and we were taking our leave, he grasped my hand in both of his. 'I worked on Indian railways for thirty-four years,' he said 'and I have been curator here for the past ten. Never before have I had the honour to meet the descendant of one of our great pioneers. I can tell you, Sir, that you have made my day.' He certainly made an unforgettable one for us.

Appendix I

THE EAST INDIAN RAILWAY

THE East Indian Railway (EIR) and the Great India Peninsular Railway (GIPR) were formed in the mid-1840s, rather shakily, with the object of building the first experimental railways in India, these to be based upon Calcutta and Bombay respectively. It was not however until August 1849 that the two companies signed contracts with the East India Company (known as the Honourable Company). Although these agreements contained much else, their main provision was that the railway companies would raise capital—in the case of the EIR about £1 million—which they would place in the hands of the East India Company, drawing upon it as necessary. The East India Company undertook to guarantee shareholders 5% interest on their money until the railways could make profits in excess of this figure.

These agreements were meant only to allow for the building of two experimental lines by EIR and GIPR and not as a policy for the future. In 1853 however the Governor General, Lord Dalhousie, issued his historic Minute to the Court of Directors of the East India Company; this set out a policy for the future of the Indian railways and was accepted by the Directors the following year. Briefly, this allowed the railway companies to raise capital and organise the construction and operation of certain lines approved by the Government—at that time the East India Company, but after its demise in 1858 the Secretary of State for India through the Viceroy. For their part the Government were to approve or

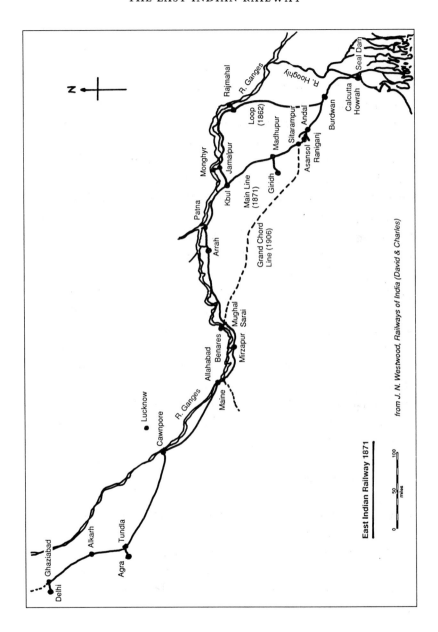

East Indian Railway 1871

from J. N. Westwood, Railways of India (David & Charles)

specify the routes and to supervise every aspect of construction, operation and accounting. The Government would continue the 5% arrangement and would also provide the necessary land without cost to the companies. The companies would carry mail free of charge and Government supplies and troops at reduced rates.

At about this time Dalhousie approved two other important measures, namely the use of a standard gauge of 5ft. 6in. and the requirement that all bridges, culverts and brickwork in the single track EIR should be built so that they would not require widening when later the line was doubled. Unfortunately, for the sake of economy, a metre and indeed other gauges were subsequently introduced on some lines, although not the EIR, so that the advantages of complete standardisation were lost.

The supervising engineers of the EIR being also responsible to the Government, it is not surprising to find that Alfred Vaux, who began his Indian career in that capacity, should have continued in Government service until his death in 1873. He had by then achieved the professional position of Under-Secretary of State for Railways.

Surveying began on the EIR as soon as the Company was formed in 1849. This was for the 121-mile experimental section to run from Calcutta to the coalfields at Raniganj—a project heartily encouraged by the P & O Steamship Company—but it was always intended that this should later become part of a trunk line from Calcutta to Bombay. Indeed, the contract for an extension to Delhi was signed in 1854, before even the experimental section had been completed. That was the year in which the first trains began operating, on the 24-mile section from Howrah to Hooghly. It had been decided against starting the line in Calcutta itself as this would have meant beginning with the construction of a major bridge across the River Hooghly. So the first station was sited at Howrah on the west bank of the river, and there the terminus was to remain.

When in January 1856 Alfred Vaux arrived in Rajmahal the line to Raniganj had been open for almost a year. Work was now proceeding on what was known as 'The Loop', running from Burdwan north to Rajmahal, thence west parallel to the bank of the Ganges as far as Kiul. The commemorative medal (see page 107) showed that the line reached Rajmahal in 1860, and it was through to Delhi by 1864—a distance of 1,130 miles. In the meantime work had started on what became known as the 'Main Line' running directly from Raniganj to Kiul which it reached in 1871, thus shortening the distance from Calcutta to Delhi by 200 miles. In 1867 a branch from Allahabad linked hands with the Indian Midland at Jabalpur, thus at last achieving the Bombay–Calcutta connection.

It is recorded that by 1868 the EIR had built 1,350 miles of railway, far more than any of the other companies, the nearest rival being the GIPR with 875 miles. This remarkable progress should not be taken as an indication that the EIR had an easy task. Although there were none of the major inclines and *ghats* which hindered the work of some of the other companies there were compensating difficulties. Apart from white ant-infested wooden sleepers and those of cast iron which were dropped and shattered before they had been laid, there were elephants who broke down telegraph poles, and tigers and wolves who terrorised the labourers. Nearly everyone suffered from malaria most of the time. Above all there were the monsoon floods and deviations of the great rivers which meant that, to be on the safe side, bridges had often to be of exaggerated length. In the EIR's part of Bengal there was no worthwhile building stone and local bricks were of poor quality. The EIR engineers therefore set up their own brickworks, but for the most part bridges were of steel girders which had to be laboriously brought up the river by steamer. The EIR's great railway workshop at Jamalpur, where it still is, was said to have been located there because its remote desolation was such that the attention of the employees would be concentrated on their work rather than on socialising. Indeed, in one of her letters Emily Vaux expressed Alfred's concern for the welfare of these people and her own scorn for the clergyman who refused to hold a service for them unless he was given a train to get there. In fact the reasons for siting the workshop in that situation were more likely to be that neighbouring Monghyr had deepwater quays alongside a part of the river which was not vulnerable to sudden changes of course, and that the area contained a local population traditionally skilled in working with metal.

Each of the railway companies made different arrangements for organising its work. Some brought in British engineering contractors and in one case the company made use of its own engineers controlling local labour. The EIR divided its line into sections, entrusting each to an Indian contractor who was supposed to be best able to cope with local conditions. This policy proved only partly successful. From the beginning the company's own engineers had had to undertake all major construction themselves, but even so many of the Indian contractors found their tasks beyond them, falling behind schedule or even going bankrupt, so that a number of sections had to be taken over entirely by the company's engineers. Alfred Vaux complains rather bitterly about this, considering that he should have been paid for the extra work. The EIR and the Delhi Railway suffered more than the other companies from the effect of the Mutiny of 1857, as Alfred describes so vividly, but they seem to have picked up their interrupted work afterwards surprisingly quickly. The siege of 'the little house at Arrah', a tale also recounted by Alfred, was the subject of romantic accounts published in England. In this case the heroes had been railwaymen rather than soldiers.

Note: I am indebted to J. N. Westwood from whose book *Railways of India* (David & Charles), I have extracted most of the essential facts given in the above Appendix.

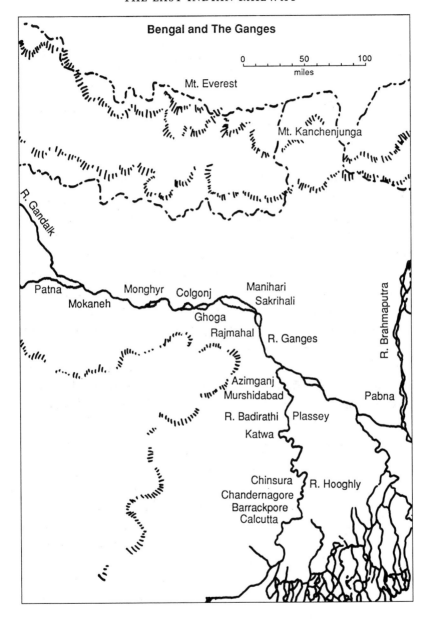

Bengal and The Ganges

Appendix II

THE INSTITUTION OF CIVIL ENGINEERS

IN 1865 Mr George Turnbull, Chief Engineer of the EIR, proposed Alfred Vaux for admission to the Institution of Civil Engineers in London, saying in part, 'In 1851 he entered the service of Mr William Dargan and was engaged in large works on the Irish Railways until 1855, when he entered the service of the East Indian Railway and was Resident engineer in large works under Mr Turnbull; he is now engaged on the maintenance and extension works of same under Mr Richard Boyle.' Mr Boyle, the District Engineer, seconded the proposal and Alfred Vaux was elected into the Institution on 6 February 1866.

Volume 27 (1867–8) of the Minutes of the Proceedings of the Institution of Civil Engineers records that the Institution considered the matter of Fresh-water Floods of Rivers. To this Alfred made the following contribution:

> Mr A. H. Vaux observed, through the Secretary, that the importance of possessing a useful means by which to classify rivers was especially apparent in Bengal in 1866 when, at the beginning of July, a remarkable flood occurred in Beerbhoom, causing much damage to the country, and temporarily obstructing the traffic of the East Indian Railway, by injuring its under works. While assisting the Chief Engineer in preparing a report to the Directors, he endeavoured to classify the different rivers which the East Indian Railway crossed, and for which the sufficiency of the waterway given was doubted. These were all

the southern tributary streams of the River Ganges, between Allahabad and Calcutta, 600 miles. Great difficulties were encountered in the attempt, as in any classification it was necessary to ascertain the area drained, the mean and exceptional amount of rainfall, and the quantity of water carried off by each river; and no certain information could be obtained on any of these points. The drainage basin could not be accurately defined, because not only did the watershed on the surface differ from the line of watershed geologically considered, but the flood itself caused grave changes in the direction of the rivers. Dams constructed for irrigation purposes were, in some instances, swept away; again, masses of trees or the debris of villages were arrested in their downward progress, and caused natural dams sufficient to divert the rivers into channels differing from those in which they formerly ran, and even occasionally throwing the whole body of a second river into the channel of one which appeared to have a totally different drainage basin. It was thus impossible to say at what point rain, which fell on certain hills, flowed into the main Ganges. The difficulty of obtaining accurate registers of the amount of rainfall daily over even a small area must have struck most engineers, and of course, in the case in question, where the rivers drained areas varying from 20 square miles to 20,000 square miles, the difficulty was greatly enhanced. A gauge situated at Soorey, at the foot of some wooded hills, registered, according to the observation of the civil surgeon of the station, 50 inches of rain in forty-eight hours; but probably rain fell more heavily in other adjacent places, where the mean fall might not perhaps exceed 70 inches in the year. Though the areas drained and the amount of rainfall were thus undefined, the Resident Engineers endeavoured to ascertain the quantity of water which passed the railway. Here again they were baffled; they knew accurately the width of opening of the bridges, but in spite of the vast volume of water surging round them, they were able to approximate only to the surface velocity at which the water passed, and they were quite unable to measure the depth of the flood. In the dry weather the rivers were rivulets flowing over fine sand. This was disturbed as the flood rose, and the beds of the rivers were quickly torn away to an uncertain depth, by a torrent running at 10 miles an hour (or nearly 15 feet per second). No soundings could be taken while these violent floods continued, and when the velocity moderated the bottom of the river was found to be again silted up. As a simple instance of a river difficult to gauge, mention might be made of the Keeul, which drained a definite basin of 1,100 square miles of hilly land, was not liable to inundate its margin, and flowed through a well-marked channel, until it reached the East Indian Railway, which crossed it by nine spans, each 150 feet; the piers being founded on wells sunk through deep sand. Here the water came down suddenly, and while the fresh lasted, the depths could not be measured.

It was to be hoped that Engineers who had had opportunities of observing 'the relation of fresh-water floods of rivers to the physical features of their basins' would take this opportunity, for the sake of their brethren who practised in countries but little known, to record their experience as to the effect which flowing water of different depths and speeds had upon different subjacent soils. Published experiments appeared invariably to give too optimistic a value to the power of water to move sand and light clay. Rivers flowed at fair speed through countries formed of even the lightest alluvial soil, and yet varied their course but slightly. A speed of 2 and 3 feet per second did not seem to be a destructive rate over light clay.